Christianity:
Key Beliefs
and Traditions

Barnabas
in
Schools

Barnabas for Children® is a registered word mark and the logo is a registered device mark of The Bible Reading Fellowship.

Text copyright © Cavan Wood 2013
Illustrations copyright © Mark Brierley 2013
The author asserts the moral right to be identified as the author of this work

Published by
The Bible Reading Fellowship
15 The Chambers, Vineyard
Abingdon OX14 3FE
United Kingdom
Tel: +44 (0)1865 319700
Email: enquiries@brf.org.uk
Website: www.brf.org.uk
BRF is a Registered Charity

ISBN 978 0 85746 251 0

First published 2013
10 9 8 7 6 5 4 3 2 1 0

Acknowledgments
Unless otherwise stated, scripture quotations are taken from the Contemporary English Version © American Bible Society 1991, 1992, 1995. Used by permission/Anglicisations © British and Foreign Bible Society 1997.

Scripture quotations taken from The Holy Bible, New International Version (Anglicised edition) are copyright © 1979, 1984, 2011 by Biblica (formerly International Bible Society). Used by permission of Hodder & Stoughton Publishers, an Hachette UK company. All rights reserved. 'NIV' is a registered trademark of Biblica (formerly International Bible Society). UK trademark number 1448790.

Cover photos: top row: © iStockphoto/Thinkstock; middle row (left to right): © Brand X Pictures/Thinkstock, © Hemera/Thinkstock, © iStockphoto/Thinkstock; bottom row (left to right): © iStockphoto/Thinkstock, © Hemera/Thinkstock; background © Hemera/Thinkstock

The paper used in the production of this publication was supplied by mills that source their raw materials from sustainably managed forests. Soy-based inks were used in its printing and the laminate film is biodegradable.

A catalogue record for this book is available from the British Library

Printed in Singapore by Craft Print International Ltd

Christianity: Key Beliefs and Traditions

An RE resource for teaching Christianity at Key Stage 2

Cavan Wood

Contents

✣

Foreword

A pupil in an RE lesson asks of the story of Christianity: 'Miss, how do we know if it's true?'

The teacher's reply really matters: should she say, 'It has been proved by scholars' or 'We don't know it's true' or 'It doesn't matter' or 'Maybe it is true for you'? It's not simple.

There is a saying of Jesus in John's Gospel: 'You will know the truth, and the truth will set you free' (John 8:32, NIV). For those who are interested in Christian education, it might be a key text. A school exists for the pursuit of truth in community: children and their teachers together try to find out what is true, and understand it. When it comes to RE, the teaching and impact of the Christian faith on the human race is undeniable, and it can be tempting to evade the truth question: 'Well, lots of people think it is important...'

In this book, author and teacher of RE Cavan Wood presents some creative and thoughtful signposts towards the answer to this question. Teachers will like the book for its practical and well-thought-out ideas about how children can engage with, reflect on and respond to the key ideas and stories of the Christian faith. RE lessons, done this way, will not panic teachers into over-hasty philosophical dismissal of pupils' deep questions. Nor will this book encourage simplistic promotion of Christianity in an unthinking way. Instead, Cavan Wood's approach will enable the teacher more confidently to encourage children to ask questions, and then to seek for answers themselves.

Perhaps the best answer to the question 'How do we know it is true?' is this one: 'Great question, Sharon. That's what we are here to find out. How do you suggest we start?' Then the RE lesson becomes the pursuit of truth, together, in community. Cavan Wood's carefully written, classroom friendly and fresh book will help teachers to develop the best kind of RE lessons.

Lat Blaylock, RE Adviser with *RE Today*

✝

Introduction

Teaching Christianity is more of a challenge than ever before. In the past, the teacher could rely on children having some basic understanding of key Christian ideas, as many would have had an encounter with the faith via church attendance.

Many would say that we are now in a post-Christian society. Although we still have some of the indications of a Christian society, and although 59 per cent of people identified themselves as Christian in the 2011 UK census, there is often little understanding of what it means to be a Christian. There may be misunderstandings of the nature of Christian events and the significance of the language used to describe faith. There are, in my experience, many pupils who would like to believe that Good Friday commemorates the day when Jesus rose from the dead, as it does not seem logical to call the day on which a person died a 'good' day—and they have a point! In a 2012 survey by BBC's *Newsround*, only 55 per cent of children knew the words of the Lord's Prayer.

We need to think about communicating a faith that is, in some ways, as alien to young people as any other faith they do not share. The idea that we need to focus on other faiths, because children already understand the traditional faith of the UK, is wrong: we need to teach all faiths as if they understood none. We also need to think about how we can improve the teaching of Christianity, as the right desire to teach other faiths during the last 40 years has perhaps meant that less time and resources have been put into keeping the teaching methodologies up to date for this particular faith.

This book is designed to give the teacher an understanding of the key Christian concepts, together with some teaching ideas for use with Key Stage 2 or early Key Stage 3. I hope that you will find some new ideas to refresh you in your teaching. I have also given links to other curriculum areas, so that you can use some of the material to help the project-based approach that many primary schools use in order to develop learning.

We need to try to understand the element of 'strangeness' in the Christian faith, as perceived by an increasing number of our children. Let us use it constructively to build their sense of mystery and enquiry.

A brief guide to Christianity

Christianity grew out of the Jewish religion, Judaism, in the first century AD. Christians believed that Jesus Christ was the Son of God—God in human form, sent to bring God and human beings back together, because sin (the evil that people do to both God and humans) had divided them. Originally, humans had had an ideal relationship with God, as the story of the garden of Eden shows, but this had broken down due to human disobedience.

Christians saw Jesus' birth as the fulfilment of the prophecies about a Messiah, a religious king who would rule with justice. Jesus' teaching, parables and miracles all pointed to the beginning of a new period—the time of the kingdom of God, when human hearts would be ruled by God. Jesus' care for women, people of different nationalities and those regarded as 'sinners' did not make him popular with the religious leaders of his day. After three years of travelling and training his disciples, he arrived for his final visit to Jerusalem during the week of Passover (the most important festival of the Jewish year, commemorating the exodus from Egypt). On the Thursday, he held a special meal for his followers, which became the basis of the Holy Communion service still practised in churches today. Later that night, Jesus was arrested and put on trial. Though originally charged with blasphemy, he was presented to the Roman governor Pontius Pilate as a political rebel, and Pilate arranged for him to be crucified on the Friday.

After six hours on the cross, Jesus died. His secret disciples Joseph and Nicodemus arranged for him to be placed in a tomb. On the Sunday morning, when some women visited the tomb, they claimed to have seen him alive. For the next six weeks, the disciples and others claimed to have seen the risen Jesus. Then, they believed, Jesus ascended to heaven.

Over the next 30 years, Christianity spread throughout the Roman Empire and is now the largest religion in the world. In its earliest years, leaders such as Paul and Peter founded churches and wrote letters to them. Within 300 years, the Christian church had formalised its ideas in a creed (a statement of belief) and had added to the Jewish scriptures to produce a Bible comprising both Old and New Testaments.

Over the centuries, the church developed different styles of worship and began to disagree about some teachings and ceremonies, leading to divisions. In the 16th century, the church was divided between Catholic believers (who followed the leadership of the Pope) and Protestant (who believed that the Bible, not the words of any leader, is the key to all belief). Other types of Christian groupings emerged over the centuries, including the Orthodox and Pentecostal churches.

At the beginning of the 21st century, Christianity finds itself side-by-side with a multiplicity of alternative faiths as well as the 'new atheists', who believe that religion, by definition, is damaging to people.

Key questions

We are going to look at Christianity—what it is about and how it can help us to live as people today. Even if we are not religious, our study will help us to think about these key questions:

- Is there a God?
- If there is, what is God like?
- How did the universe get here and does it have any purpose?
- How did human beings get here?
- What is the meaning of my life?
- Why is there evil in the world?

- Why do both good and bad people suffer?
- How can we tell right from wrong?
- Is there life after death? Does something of me survive death?
- Will I meet people who have died before me?
- Did Jesus perform miracles? If he did not, what do all those stories about him mean? Are they symbolic?
- Why did Jesus use parables to teach people? Why did they irritate so many people in his day?
- Why did Jesus end up dying on a cross when he seemed to be teaching things that many non-religious people think are wise?
- Did he rise from the dead?
- If he did rise, where is he now?
- Did the early Christians die for something they knew was a lie?
- What is the Church all about?
- Why is the Bible important to Christians today?
- Why do ceremonies matter to Christians?
- How should I treat other people and what does Christianity have to say to help me in my relationships with them?

The purpose of this book is to help the class think through their responses to these questions. It is important to have a questioning mind, to be like a detective and see the possibilities of answers different from the ones that we might immediately give.

How to use this book

The material in this book is intended to be adaptable. Although I have designed each section with learning objectives, you should not be limited by them. Each section contains a selection of material that you can use to develop into more than one lesson if you prefer. Worksheets and activity-related illustrations are available to download at www.barnabasinschools.org.uk/extra-resources/.

✛

Creation: how did the universe get here?

Learning objectives

- All pupils will be able to explain the Christian idea of creation.
- Most pupils will be able to compare the Christian idea of creation with other beliefs about how the universe began.
- Some pupils will be able to develop their own detailed responses to the different ideas about how the universe began and evaluate how those ideas affect people's behaviour.

Starter

Ask pupils to imagine that they could ask God three questions about the way the earth and the universe are. What would they be? What answers might God give?

Introduction

'In the beginning God created the heavens and the earth' is the powerful opening phrase of the book of Genesis. It is one that has had people debating fiercely for the last 200 years.

The Bible story about creation is a very positive one. Everything that is made has been made on purpose and is described by God as being either 'good' or 'very good'. Compare that view with this one:

The story so far: In the beginning, the Universe was created. This has made a lot of people very angry and was widely regarded as a bad move.
THE RESTAURANT AT THE END OF THE UNIVERSE, DOUGLAS ADAMS

Which is right—the positive view of creation or the more negative one? What do you think? Ask pupils to talk about it with a partner and then share their answers with another partner.

 Activity

Write and/or draw a creation story about a world or universe coming into existence. It could be the one we live in or another one that they have made up.

The story should explain how this world/universe came into existence. Was there a god or gods or other types of being involved? Does the world/universe have a purpose, a meaning? If it does, what is it?

Creation stories often try to explain why pain and evil are in the world. Pupils should try to do this in their stories.

The creation stories should include some labelled drawings or diagrams related to the story. Pupils can use a computer or, if they prefer, they can produce a storyboard. Below are some sentence stems to help them get going with a storyboard.

- My world/universe was created by…
- The first thing to be created was…
- The last thing to be created was…
- The meaning of the world/universe I created is…
- There is pain in my world/universe because…
- Evil things happen in my world/universe because…
- I would make sure that in my universe…

Cross-curricular links

- Art: examine pictures of creation by famous artists.
- Design and Technology: consider the design process and how it could be applied to the story of creation.
- Music: listen to pieces connected to creation, such as Moby's 'God moving over the face of the waters' or *The Creation* by Haydn.

Assembly/Reflection

How might a belief that the world has a purpose alter the way in which we treat it? The idea of creation is that this world is special and we have an important role to play in it. How could we show this in our lives?

✢

In the image of the Father

Learning objectives

- All pupils will be able to explain the idea of humans being made in the image of God.
- Most pupils will be able to explain how the idea of the image of God influences belief and behaviour.
- Some pupils will be able to reflect on how this may or may not be of benefit.

Starter

Ask pupils to draw an image of themselves on a piece of paper while keeping their eyes shut. What do they draw? Normally, they will come up with a distorted image of themselves. Ask them why they think they have drawn themselves as they have.

Introduction

At the beginning of the Bible, we read this: 'So God created humans to be like himself; he made men and women' (Genesis 1:27).

What makes a good parent? There are all kinds of qualities that people might talk about. A good parent needs to show love, care and a willingness to be selfless on behalf of their children, to listen and to support them in difficult times.

If only every parent was this good! But parents are human. They make mistakes and say and do the wrong things. Yet, at their best, they can be major forces for good in their children's lives.

How far are people like their parents? What exactly does it mean to be 'in the image of God'? Is it a good thing to be like God? To be made in the image of God can mean many things, but would include the following:

- Humans, like God, are spiritual beings. Something about us can survive death.
- Humans, like God, can show and give love.
- Humans, like God, can be creative.

The Italian author Carlo Collodi wrote the story *The Adventures of Pinocchio* in which a puppet wishes to become human. At the end of the story, a fairy grants his wish:

He went to look in the mirror, but he could not recognise himself. Instead of the usual picture of a wooden puppet, he saw the expressive, intelligent face of a good-looking boy, with brown hair and blue eyes, who looked contented and full of joy.

You might like to use the following piece of drama to help your class explore this idea.

A dialogue about who you are

Voice 1:   They say that you are what you eat.

Voice 2:   They say that you are what you say.

Voice 1:   They say that you are what you see in the mirror.

Voice 2:   But what if the mirror is a distorting mirror?

Voice 1:   What if the way I look in the mirror has become influenced by what other people tell me I should see, rather than what is actually there?

Voice 2:   So who is the real you? The one you see in the mirror? The one that you think you look like?

Voice 1:   So often, when we look at a photograph of ourselves, we refuse to believe that the image we see *is* ourselves.

Voice 2:   The image makes us too fat, too slim, too short or too tall to be truly us.

Voice 1:   We might say that the person who took the photo-graph failed to capture our 'good side'.

Voice 2:   But will these lies do? Shouldn't we tell the truth to ourselves?

Voice 1:   Does it really matter what a person looks like?

Voice 2:   Shouldn't it matter more that they know how to show love to others?

Voice 1:   Shouldn't we judge not by the cover of the book but what we find inside when we read it—get to know the person to see what the reality is?

Voice 2:   Can we see the truth of a person in their face, in the way they stand, in their handshake? Perhaps we need time to really understand who we are and what other people are like.

Voice 2:   The face, the look, might give us a first impression, but that can be wrong.

Voice 1:   The face might not tell us all.

Voice 2:   Beauty might be in the eye of the beholder, but so might the ability to distort things.

Thoughts about the image of God

You can use the following reading in class or as part of an assembly that links to the theme you are studying.

We can greatly limit people by our judgment of what they look like. In his great speech against racism, 'I have a dream', Martin Luther King said that he wanted his children to be 'judged by the content of their character, not by the colour of their skin'. We might not judge people by their skin colour, but are we guilty sometimes of putting a person into a category, saying that we won't like or trust that person because of their way of dressing or the way they look?

If we do it to others, we might also do it to ourselves. We can cause ourselves so much unnecessary pain when we think that, to be complete or better people, we need to look or dress in a particular way. Forget it! We are unique. Not one person has exactly the same fingerprint as another, so why, if we can cope with that, do we feel that we will only be accepted if we do or seem to be one thing?

We need to realise that each one of us is a unique and wonderful human being. No person will look completely like you. No one has had the influences or the friendships you will have.

We need to see the strengths that we have and to realise that people's thoughts about what is beautiful or attractive may not last. Think about the way hairstyles change over the years—short, long, wavy, straight... The outside of a person might give us some information about them, or even help us to understand something about who they are, but it is not and never will be the whole story.

On the TV programme *Britain's Got Talent*, a woman called Susan Boyle appeared and the judges thought that she looked quite ordinary. Then she started singing and she had a great voice. Whatever we look like, each one of us has talents that will help us to realise that there is more to life than looks. The idea of the image of God inside us shows that we are all capable of being creative and reflecting God's qualities.

⊕ Activity

In the past, one way in which families tried to express their values was through a shield that had symbols on it and possibly a motto to display their family's key aspiration.

Show a shield divided into four parts. Tell the pupils that they are to fill the four parts with key symbols that express who they are. They should also try to write a motto of not more than six words that communicates a key truth about them.

For example, if I were do to this for myself, my shield might include:

- A picture of my family
- A bookshelf (I love books!)
- A symbol for school
- An image linked to key things that I believe in

My motto would be something like 'Have faith, show love', as this expresses two key values I feel that I have.

Be open with the class about what might be on your shield. You could construct a shield based on things that other members of staff have told you, perhaps turning it into a guessing game. (Make sure that other staff members are happy for their information to be shared with others.)

Cross-curricular links

- PSHE: think about how we develop as people.
- Art: make shields (as above) to explore the uniqueness, creativity and originality of each person.

Assembly/Reflection

The idea of being made in the image of God tells us that everyone is special: all are important. We can be spiritual, loving and creative: how might that influence the way we treat others?

✣

Sin: passing the blame

Learning objectives

- All pupils will be able to explain the Christian idea of sin.
- Most pupils will be able to give some examples of causes of 'sinful' behaviour.
- Some pupils will be able to give an opinion as to which causes are more important than others.

Starter

Elton John sang a song called 'Sorry seems to be the hardest word'. Why do you think it is so hard to say sorry? Should you say 'I'm sorry, but I…' or is that not a real apology?

Introduction

Christians believe that humans are bound to act in what they call a sinful way. To be sinful is to choose to be selfish and to go against the will of God in life.

It is easy for us to blame others for the problems and bad things in the world. Back in the 1900s, there was a writer called G.K. Chesterton who wrote to *The Times* newspaper in response to a series of letters discussing what was wrong with the world. His letter was the shortest:

Dear Sir,
   What is wrong with the world?
   I am.
Yours faithfully,
G.K. Chesterton

What do we hear in a classroom, though?

'I didn't do it—it was him/her.'
'It wasn't my fault.'
'They started it.'

People love to pass the blame. According to one of the first stories in the Bible, when Eve ate the fruit from the tree of the knowledge of good and evil (breaking the one rule that God had given), she blamed the snake for encouraging her to do so. Then, when Adam made the same mistake, he blamed Eve. Saying sorry and admitting we have done wrong is very difficult: we often want to find a way out of admitting we were wrong.

Compare this attitude with the words of the former president of the USA, Harry S. Truman, who had a notice on his desk that said, 'The buck stops here!' The notice meant he would take full responsibility for everything that happened in the country.

Christians believe that each person is responsible for their own actions and the consequences of those actions. This belief affects their relationships with other people and, above all, with God. They believe that their bad actions and thoughts can cut them off from God, as if there is a wall or barrier separating them from God. They call these bad actions and thoughts 'sin'. This word came from a term in archery that describes a person missing the target with their arrow: sin means being less of the person that Christians believe God wants us to be.

⊕ Activity

Using the information in this section, invite pupils to devise a 'Pass the Blame' board game. The game will need to include questions, chance cards, dice and counters. Pupils should work with at least one other person so that they can plan together how to make the most effective game.

Help pupils to get started by showing them a selection of board games. One that might be helpful is Snakes and Ladders. The snake could represent passing the blame to someone else, and the ladder could represent a person being prepared to take the blame for something they were responsible for.

 Activity

Devise a drama on the theme of passing the blame. Ask the class to think through the consequences of not accepting responsibility for an action.

 Activity

Write a poem that explores the idea of sin and how it affects people.

Cross-curricular links

- PSHE: explore the question of guilt and responsibility. (This theme could be picked up in circle time.)
- Drama: Create a drama on the idea of passing the blame (as above).

Assembly/Reflection

It is important to admit when we have done wrong and to be able to say sorry. How can we make sure that we do both of these things?

✢

The Ten Commandments: what are the rules?

Learning objectives

- All pupils will be able to explain the importance of the Ten Commandments for Christians.
- Most pupils will be able to think about the relevance of the Ten Commandments to today's world.
- Some pupils will be able to begin to devise some alternative commandments of their own, with reasons to justify them.

Starter

Pose some or all of the following questions. Ask your class to work in groups to produce responses to them.

- How could you play a board game with no rules?
- What problems might the absence of rules cause for people trying to play the game?
- What is the difference between a rule and a promise?
- What if we got rid of all school rules?
- Think of five rules that you might encourage people to follow so that they and their friends can live the best life possible.
- How easy do you find it to follow or keep a rule?
- Is it easier to keep a promise?
- Why do rules matter to Christians?

Introduction

Most of us do not like rules, yet they are important. School rules help us to know how we should and should not treat people. We need rules for motorists and other users of the road so that we know how to stay safe. Most electronic items come with an instruction booklet to help us to use them as they should be used, so that they work properly.

Jews and Christians believe that the Ten Commandments were rules given by God to Moses, to help people live lives that would please God and help them to be the best people that they could be. For many Christians, these commandments are so important that they are displayed in churches where everyone can see them and remember their importance. How many of the commandments should still matter today, in a world where so many people are not Christians?

Here are the Ten Commandments that are contained in the Bible.

God said to the people of Israel:

I am the Lord your God, the one who brought you out of Egypt where you were slaves.

Do not worship any god except me.

Do not make idols that look like anything in the sky or on earth or in the sea under the earth. Don't bow down and worship idols. I am the Lord your God, and I demand all your love. If you reject me, I will punish your families for three or four generations. But if you love me and obey my laws, I will be kind to your families for thousands of generations.

Do not misuse my name. I am the Lord your God, and I will punish anyone who misuses my name.

Remember that the Sabbath Day belongs to me. You have six days when you can do your work, but the seventh day of each week belongs to me, your God. No one is to work on that day—

not you, your children, your slaves, your animals, or the foreigners who live in your towns. In six days I made the sky, the earth, the seas, and everything in them, but on the seventh day I rested. That's why I made the Sabbath a special day that belongs to me.

Respect your father and your mother, and you will live a long time in the land I am giving you.

Do not murder.

Be faithful in marriage.

Do not steal.

Do not tell lies about others.

Do not want… anything that belongs to someone else. Don't want… anyone's house, wife or husband, slaves, oxen, donkeys or anything else.

EXODUS 20:1–17

Are any of these commandments surprising?

These rules have been followed for over 3000 years by Jews and Christians, and have also been an influence on Muslims as well as people of no faith. They have helped to shape the laws of many countries.

You might think that they fall into two categories: religious laws (the first four) and social laws that could apply to religious and non-religious people alike. But this is not how religious people see them: they are all equally important and should be lived out. There are another 603 laws in the Old Testament, which Orthodox Jewish people try to follow as well as these ten, but many other Jews and Christians think that only these ten are ultimately binding: the other laws are there to help us think about how we could live a good life and make sure we have the best type of society.

Ask pupils to discuss with a partner which commandments they think are still important and why. Can they come to a conclusion?

The class might try to come up with answers to the following questions.

- Can you have a law that is about the way people think rather than the way they act? (The tenth commandment is about the way people think rather than act.)
- Which of the Ten Commandments are still parts of our law today?
- Which commandment do you think is the most important and why?
- Which do you think is the least important and why?

 Activity

Work with a partner to write a list of the ten most important commandments for our time. Which might need to be lost from the original list? Which might stay in? What rules are not mentioned in the list but would seem good to add? Make sure that pupils are able to give reasons for their choices.

Here are some other questions to think about.

- Could you have a country without any rules?
- Are there too many rules? Are there too few?
- How could you tell a good rule from a bad rule?

Cross-curricular links

- PSHE: talk about rule-setting.
- Citizenship: explore laws, communities and their moral codes.
- Critical thinking: practise making and justifying choices.

Assembly/Reflection

We might often think that rules are not very helpful, but they can help us to know how to behave and they can stop us from hurting others by design or by accident. What rules do you have in your school, and how do they help people?

Prophecy: learning to live now, thinking about the future

Learning objectives

- All pupils will be able to explain the idea of prophecy.
- Most pupils will be able to explain how the idea of prophecy has inspired people to think differently about the world.
- Some pupils will be able to explain how the idea of prophecy helps people to assess what needs to change.

Starter

Pose some or all of these questions for the class to think about, working in pairs.

- What do you not like about the world we live in?
- What needs to change?
- How might this change come about?

Introduction

People have always thought about what might happen in the future. Sometimes these ideas can be exciting, looking forward to a better world, but sometimes we might imagine a nightmare of how the world might be threatened or go wrong in some way. Some films and books try to tell us about the future. Science fiction writers, for example, have dreamed of meeting aliens, travelling to the stars and moving through time. Many have written about a paradise, a place where all things are perfect, or of a time when everything will be at peace.

Here are the words of the prophet Isaiah, who shared a vision of a better world that he thought could come into being:

Leopards will lie down with young goats,
and wolves will rest with lambs.
Calves and lions will eat together
and be cared for by little children.
Cows and bears will share the same pasture;
their young will rest side by side.
Lions and oxen will both eat straw.

Little children will play near snake holes.
They will stick their hands
into dens of poisonous snakes
and never be hurt.

Nothing harmful will take place
on the Lord's holy mountain.
Just as water fills the sea,
the land will be filled with people
who know and honour the Lord.
ISAIAH 11:1–9

It would have been impossible for all these different types of animals to live together—but that's the point. Isaiah is saying that this isn't going to be achieved by human beings, but God will make it happen.

According to the *Oxford English Dictionary*, the word 'prophecy' means 'the foretelling or prediction of what is to come' or 'something that is declared by a prophet, especially a divinely inspired prediction, instruction or exhortation', or 'a divinely inspired utterance or revelation'.

Look at the following part of the speech 'I have a dream' by Martin Luther King, where he uses language from the biblical prophets to help him make a case for the end of racism in the USA:

I have a dream that one day every valley shall be exalted, every hill and mountain shall be made low, the rough places will be made plain, and the crooked places will be made straight, and the glory of the Lord shall be revealed, and all flesh shall see it together.

This is our hope. This is the faith with which I return to the South. With this faith we will be able to hew out of the mountain of despair a stone of hope. With this faith we will be able to transform the jangling discords of our nation into a beautiful symphony of brotherhood. With this faith we will be able to work together, to pray together, to struggle together, to go to jail together, to stand up for freedom together, knowing that we will be free one day.

This will be the day when all of God's children will be able to sing with a new meaning, 'My country, 'tis of thee, sweet land of liberty, of thee I sing. Land where my fathers died, land of the pilgrim's pride, from every mountainside, let freedom ring.'

 Activity

Explore the ideas in the 'I have a dream' speech and create a mime to explain some of its key ideas.

Cross-curricular links

- English: discover stories about different and better worlds than our own.
- History: explore the idea of what makes a just or fair society and examine in what ways our society may have become more just. Think about how the idea of a 'promised land' can lead to both improvements and tensions in countries.

Assembly/Reflection

Prophecy is all about seeing things that are wrong in the world and then thinking about how they could be put right. What could we do in our school, our family and our local area to make life better for others and ourselves?

The Messiah: a special king from God

Learning objectives

- All pupils will be able to explain the idea of a messiah.
- Most pupils will be able to develop their own views on what makes a good leader.
- Some pupils will be able to explain how the idea of a messiah has been applied to Jesus, being able to give their own views on whether or not he does show the relevant qualities.

Starter

Invite the class to think about these questions with a partner:

- What makes a person a good leader?
- What makes a person a bad leader?
- Which of the qualities of a good leader do you have?
- In what ways are you a leader?
- What leaders do you see that you would like to follow?

Introduction

People want different qualities in a leader. Some want leaders to be strong enough to take tough decisions. Some want them to be good listeners or good team players. Others think it is important for leaders to be prepared to stand out from the crowd.

Leaders might need different skills for their particular role. A prime minister or president does not need all the same talents as a football captain, although there might be some overlap. A teacher does not need exactly the same qualities as a parent. A Scout or Guide leader might have different skills from a police officer. Kings and queens were seen as good leaders in the past not necessarily because they had any particular skill but because they were able to claim that God had put them in charge.

Sometimes leaders bring with them great expectation for change and can then cause great disappointment. To be a leader is to risk disappointment, perhaps to let people down.

For many centuries, the Jewish people dreamed of a great king who would help the nation become a place of peace. Early in their history, they had a king called David, whom they remembered as a very special leader. Although he had made some mistakes, they longed for another leader like him to help them deal with difficult times. This hoped-for leader was the 'Messiah', the 'anointed one' who would be chosen by God to make things better.

As the idea developed, the Messiah came to be seen not just as another David but also as a person who would have a special relationship with God and his people. The prophets talked about this king and, for Christians, Jesus became the person who made all of these promises and predictions come true. They felt that there was no need for another messiah: all the promises had come true in the life of Jesus.

Look at these two quotations from the book of the prophet Isaiah. They tell us about what the Messiah should be like. You will sometimes hear this reading at Christmas, as many Christians believe that Isaiah was predicting the birth of Jesus and what sort of person he would be.

A child has been born for us.
We have been given a son who will be our ruler.
His names will be Wonderful Adviser and Mighty God,
Eternal Father and Prince of Peace.
His power will never end; peace will last for ever.

He will rule David's kingdom and make it grow strong.
He will always rule with honesty and justice.
The Lord All-Powerful will make certain that all of this is done.
ISAIAH 9:6–7

Here is my servant!
I have made him strong.
He is my chosen one; I am pleased with him.
I have given him my Spirit,
and he will bring justice to the nations.
He won't shout or yell or call out in the streets.
He won't break off a bent reed or put out a dying flame,
but he will make sure that justice is done.
He won't stop or give up until he brings justice
everywhere on earth,
and people in foreign nations long for his teaching.
ISAIAH 42:1–4

Activity

Write a job description for the Messiah. Do you think it is possible to find a leader who will please everyone?

Activity

Draw a series of pictures to show the idea of a messiah.

Cross-curricular links

• Citizenship: research leadership and systems of government.

Assembly/Reflection

What makes a good leader? How could we be a good example to someone else? Which role models should we try to follow and why?

✝

The Trinity: Father, Son and Holy Spirit

Learning objectives

- All pupils will be able to explain what Christians mean by the Trinity.
- Most pupils will be able to explain how an understanding of the Trinity might influence Christian behaviour.
- Some pupils will be able to explain how an understanding of the Trinity influences Christian behaviour, especially when thinking about the church as a community.

Starter

Invite pupils to look at these pictures.

What links all three images? The answer is that they are all forms of water. One is a liquid (the puddle), one is a gas (the steam) and one is a solid (the ice cube).

Introduction

Christians believe that God is one, but can be known in three ways, as the Father, the Son and the Holy Spirit. They believe that God is a trinity—three persons, but still one God, each with a special role. The Father is the part of God who brought the universe into being. The Son became a human being in the person of Jesus Christ. The Holy Spirit is the part of God that can live inside human beings and was sent to all the believers at Pentecost.

We could think about this idea using maths. $1 + 1 + 1 = 3$, but if the sum is re-expressed as $1 \times 1 \times 1$, the answer is 1.

Help the class to understand that different people see us in different ways. To our teachers, we are their pupils. To our parents, we are their children. To our friends, we are their friends. We don't speak to any of these people in exactly the same way. We might tell our friends a joke that we would never tell our parents or teachers. We would not be too worried if our friend complained that we had not done our homework. Each person has a role, and each part of us responds to them in a different way.

 Activity

Think of other ways of describing the Trinity by choosing something that can be expressed in three different ways.

 Activity

One of the ideas in the Trinity is that God is like a community, a group of persons living together. Think about the communities that we belong to: family, school, local area. What benefits do we get from each of these communities? What problems might each of them cause for us?

Activity

Ask pupils to design a poster to show the different communities that they belong to and explain under each community why it is important to them.

Cross-curricular links

- Critical thinking: think about how to communicate difficult ideas.
- Citizenship: explore roles and responsibilities in the community.

Assembly/Reflection

Deep at the heart of the Trinity is the idea of the importance of a community, a family. What can we do in the school to help people feel more part of the community? What stops people feeling part of it?

✛

Christmas: the birth of Jesus

Learning objectives

- All pupils will be able to explain why Christmas is important to Christians.
- Most pupils will be able to comment on how Christmas is observed today.
- Some pupils will be able to try to decide if Jesus would approve of the festival. They will also be able to explain the idea of incarnation.

Starter

Ask the class to write down, in two minutes, as many words as possible that connect with Christmas. Highlight which words are religious and which are not religious.

Introduction

Christmas really isn't just about the presents: no, it is about a presence. Christians believe that, in Jesus, God became a human being and experienced what it was like to be a human being.

Listen to this retelling of the Christmas story, told from a minor character's point of view.

The innkeeper's wife's story

Ben and I married 20 years ago and decided that we would go into the innkeeping business. Being on the main road between Bethlehem and Jerusalem, we get a lot of pilgrims going up to the city for festivals or just to worship at the temple. We get Roman soldiers here, too. We're not too proud to take anyone's money, and they pay well.

One day we got a notice that said the Romans were going to have a census in order to update their tax records. This sounded good for business, it really did. I decided that we had better stock up on as much ale and food as we could store. Every room was dusted from top to bottom: we knew there would be so many visitors that we would need to get ready to use all the space we have.

So, a few days before the people had to do the paperwork, they began to arrive. We stood in our bedroom, looking out to the hills, watching them come down. There were hundreds of them; no, there were thousands of them, and Ben rubbed his hands. 'Think of all that profit, Ruth. We'll be able to go on that holiday you keep going on about—and more.'

He always smiled when he thought he could make a big profit.

So we filled up all the rooms quickly that day. We even had people who were prepared to sleep five in rooms meant for two. We took their money and we felt that things were going great.

Well, by the end of the day, we were tired out. Ben wanted to count the money before we went to bed, and I sat there in the inn, half asleep, watching my husband pile up coin upon coin.

Then, about midnight, there was a knock at the door. It was a young man, with an even younger woman sitting on a donkey. I was standing behind Ben when he opened the door.

'Have you got a room?' the young man asked.

Ben was cross: he is always cross when he gets tired. 'Can't you read? The notice outside says that we have no room in this inn!'

The man looked where Ben was pointing. 'No room at all?'

Ben had one of those looks he gets when one of the children

has done something very wrong. 'I told you that we have no room in this inn.'

The young man said, 'But my wife is about to give birth.'

Ben turned around to me and mouthed, 'What can I do?'

I felt that we had to help, but every room was full. Then I said, without thinking, 'What about the stable?'

First Ben looked at me as if I was mad, and then he said to the man, 'You can use the stable.'

The young man stepped up to Ben, shook his hand and then threw his arms around him.

'Thank you, thanks so much!' The young man seemed to be crying.

Ben decided that he had better take them round the back. He told me that when he got to the stable, there seemed to be a huge star above it.

'And I heard singing, like angels.' Ben wasn't given to being poetic. Angels, singing, in this part of town? It sounded unlikely.

I decided that I ought to go and help them, so I took some towels and some hot water—but by the time I got there, it was over. The baby had been born and was lying in the manger. He was asleep, and his mother was saying, 'Is he all right?'

'He is fine,' the young man said. 'Just as the angel promised.'

The angel? Perhaps there had been an angel or two singing above our stable, then.

We didn't sleep that night. We were trying to clean up the stable and make it a place where a baby could be happy.

Then there were the visitors—first, some shepherds, then some men claiming they had followed a star to find our little stable.

I asked the mother what they were going to call the boy.

She smiled. 'His name is Jesus.'

Jesus means 'the one who saves', so perhaps the sound of angels and the visits of shepherds and wise men to our little stable might be the beginning of something big, something that might change everything. Who knows?

It certainly changed Ben, as he did not charge the couple a penny. Now that alone is a miracle, believe me!

 Activity

Collect a number of Christmas cards and sort them into categories according to the pictures they show. Here are some suggestions:

- Angels
- Wise men
- Stars
- Mary and the baby Jesus
- Manger scenes

Divide pupils into groups to look at the selection of different events. What do the cards have in common? What are the differences?

Ask pupils to choose the most striking image to help them write a poem about the birth of Jesus. Here are some suggested first lines to get them going (or you can offer your own alternatives):

- When the angels came from heaven with their message…
- Wise men came to search for the baby…
- Following the star from afar…
- The mother and the child sat in silence…
- In the silence of the night, a baby cried in a barn…

Which important ideas from the story are not covered by the cards that you have looked at? Which parts of the story are covered more often than you expected? Which parts are least well covered?

Why do you think that so many Christmas cards now have pictures on them that are about the time of the year—such as robins, snowmen or log fires—rather than religious pictures? Do pupils think that this is a good or bad thing? Can they give reasons for their answers?

 Activity

We live in a culture that is dominated by advertising. We are being sold a dream—that if we eat or own a particular product, we will be much more fulfilled individuals.

Use pupils' 'advert-literacy' to help them question the underlying assumptions.

- Take some teaching of Jesus about money or possessions (for example, Matthew 6:19–21; Matthew 19:16–30, Luke 19:1–10) and then look at a selection of adverts, either in the press or from television. How do the adverts compare and contrast with the values expressed in Jesus' teaching?
- The Church of England has run various Christmas-themed adverts over the past few years. Go to www.churchads.net to see some examples. How effective are they?

Cross-curricular links

- Art: study the images of Christmas.
- English: write responsive poems about the event.
- Critical thinking: put images into categories and consider why some are used more than others.

Assembly/Reflection

Christmas is about the giving and receiving of presents, but it is so much more than that. How might we help those who are less fortunate than we are at times like Christmas?

✛

The baptism of Jesus

Learning objectives

- All pupils will be able to explain why the baptism of Jesus was a key moment in his life.
- Most pupils will be able to explain how the baptism of Jesus showed his divine origin.
- Some pupils will be able to explain important moments of change in their lives, saying in detail why they were important.

Starter

Ask pupils to think about the most important moments of their lives, show them on a timeline and share them with a partner. Why were they so important? Did pupils realise they were important at the time or only afterwards?

Introduction

One of the key turning points in the life of Jesus happened when he was about 30. As far as we know, he had lived in the town of Nazareth since he was a boy and had been making his living as a carpenter. The Gospels tell us that Jesus' cousin became known as John the Baptist. Jesus seemed convinced that he needed to be baptised by John before starting his ministry—his time of teaching and working miracles. Look at this story of the baptism of Jesus:

About that time Jesus came from Nazareth in Galilee, and John baptised him in the River Jordan. As soon as Jesus came out of the water, he saw the sky open and the Holy Spirit coming down to him like a dove. A voice from heaven said, 'You are my own dear Son, and I am pleased with you.'

MARK 1:9–11

John the Baptist was shy about baptising Jesus, as he did not feel that he was good enough to do the job. He saw in Jesus something special, something of God that made him feel unworthy.

Jesus had a key meeting with God, and the next thing we might expect is that he would go and do a miracle. Instead, we find him in the desert being questioned by a being called the devil about what he is being asked to do (Mark 1:12–13; Matthew 4:1–11). This will be the subject of the next lesson.

 Activity

Look at some of the images of the baptism of Jesus, which you can find by going online at http://photobucket.com/images/jesusbaptism. Which pictures do you like? Which don't you like? Give reasons for your answer. Create your own image of the story.

Activity

In the story of Jesus' baptism, God speaks from the sky. Why do you think a cloud is often used as a picture of God in different religions? Find out about clouds and their different shapes from a website such as www.weatherwizkids.com/weather-clouds.htm.

Cross-curricular links

- History: study key turning points in events.
- PSHE: talk about trying to be true to ourselves and seeing the value of others.
- Science: research clouds (as above).

Assembly/Reflection

Jesus' baptism was important, as it was a key milestone in his life. How can we make sure that we make the right decisions at turning points in our lives?

+

The temptation of Jesus

Learning objectives

- All pupils will be able to explain the idea of temptation.
- Most pupils will be able to explain how Jesus dealt with temptation.
- Some pupils will be able to think about how temptation affected Jesus and might affect our own behaviour.

Introduction

A few years ago, an advertisement for cream cakes called them 'naughty but nice'.

The idea of temptation is an important one to explore. Dealing with ideas and emotions that can overpower us, if we let them, is key. Many pupils seem to think that temptation is simply about whether or not to give in to more cream cakes.

What does temptation mean? The dictionary says the following: '(1) the act of tempting; enticement or allurement. (2) something that tempts, entices, or allures. (3) the fact or state of being tempted, especially to evil.'

In the story of the garden of Eden, both Adam and Eve are tempted by the snake and give in. In the story about the temptation of Jesus, something very different happens. Christians say that Jesus knew what temptation was like but he did not give in to it, and this is an encouragement and a challenge to them. The first experience that Jesus had after his baptism was a face-to-face set of temptations with the devil.

The Holy Spirit led Jesus into the desert, so that the devil could test him. After Jesus had gone without eating for forty days and nights, he was very hungry. Then the devil came to him and said, 'If you are God's Son, tell these stones to turn into bread.'

Jesus answered, 'The Scriptures say: "No one can live only on food. People need every word that God has spoken."' Next, the devil took Jesus to the holy city and made him stand on the highest part of the temple. The devil said, 'If you are God's Son, jump off. The Scriptures say: "God will give his angels orders about you. They will catch you in their arms, and you won't hurt your feet on the stones."' Jesus answered, 'The Scriptures also say, "Don't try to test the Lord your God!"' Finally, the devil took Jesus up on a very high mountain and showed him all the kingdoms on earth and their power. The devil said to him, 'I will give all this to you, if you will bow down and worship me.' Jesus answered, 'Go away Satan! The Scriptures say: "Worship the Lord your God and serve only him."'

Then the devil left Jesus, and angels came to help him.

MATTHEW 4:1–11

What were all of these temptations about?

The first temptation was to turn stones to bread. This was a way of saying that Jesus should seek his own needs above everyone else's. The second temptation was to jump off the top of the temple, a way of showing everyone how much God loved him, as he would be rescued by angels. The third temptation was to worship the devil and the idea of power itself.

Each of these temptations went to the heart of Jesus' beliefs about the sort of messiah that he should be. Jesus wanted to be the person he felt God had called him to be: humble and helpful to others, behaving more like a servant than a king.

Ask the pupils to list the things that they can be tempted to do. Here are some examples:

- To swear when they have dropped something on their foot.
- To spread gossip that they know to be untrue.

- To say something cruel about someone else's appearance.
- To go for the easiest option in life, not for one that will stretch them.

⊕ Activity

In confronting the devil, Jesus had a clear view of who he was and what he wanted to achieve. We now have enough information to create a clearer picture of Jesus.

Social networking has become important to many people, and this exercise will allow pupils to use their skills to put together a profile. Facebook has become one of the most popular of these sites. It has certain underlying design features that you could mimic if you were to use it to explore the life of a religious leader.

Here is an example:

- Name: Jesus Christ
- Place of birth: Bethlehem, Israel
- Number of friends: Twelve disciples, plus…
- Family members: Mary, Joseph, James…

If this exercise is to be done properly, you should make sure that pupils approach it seriously and do not undermine its purpose.

⊕ Activity

Many pupils will enjoy playing with trading cards. Some kinds of cards give facts and figures on subjects from football to films, pop music to dinosaurs. Create a series of similar cards about figures that are important within Christianity: Mary Magdalene, Thomas, John the Baptist and so on. Here are two examples.

- Name: Jesus Christ
- Age when he died: 33
- Method of death: On a cross

- Country of birth: Israel
- Single
- Teacher
- Parable teller
- Miracle worker

- Name: Simon Peter
- Age when he died: Unknown
- Method of death: On an upside-down cross
- Country of birth: Israel
- Married
- Fisherman
- Leader of the church in Rome

Cross-curricular links

- PSHE: think about being responsible for our own behaviour and dealing with our weaknesses.
- English: explore the power of words to help us in difficult times.

Assembly/Reflection

Temptation is about putting pressure on us to be less than we should be. What influences might make us less than good? How can we work to overcome them?

✝

Jesus the teacher

Learning objectives

- All pupils will be able to explain how Jesus was a teacher.
- Most pupils will be able to comment on his effectiveness as a teacher.
- Some pupils will be able to comment in detail on his teaching.

Starter

What qualities do good teachers have? Ask pupils to write a list and show it to a partner. Do the pupils think their partner has any of the qualities on their own list?

Introduction

Jesus had a career for three years as a travelling teacher. His way of teaching was different from that of the people around him. He often used stories (called parables) to explain his key ideas. These stories were very powerful in challenging people's thoughts about the world around them. He would frequently challenge his hearers to look at things afresh.

Jesus would also use wise sayings in order to provoke a reaction. They sometimes even had a comic edge.

For Christians, Jesus' teaching is very important. They believe that his teaching in the Gospels, especially in a section of Matthew's Gospel called the Sermon on the Mount, helps them to make decisions about what is right and wrong.

Ask pupils what influences them when they have to make decisions about what they think is right and wrong. They should try to think of at least three influences and explain why they are helpful.

Activity

The way Jesus lived his life is very important to the way Christians should live theirs. Christians believe that Jesus is a good example of someone who is loving, unselfish, prepared to speak out when things are wrong and forgiving towards other people. Some Christians wear a wristband showing the letters WWJD, which stand for 'What Would Jesus Do?' This is a way of helping that person to think about the way they live their life, so that they try to behave in line with the way they think Jesus would behave if he were there with them.

Look at these teachings of Jesus:

- 'God blesses those people who make peace' (Matthew 5:9).
- 'Love others as much as you love yourself' (Matthew 22:39).
- 'Love your enemies' (Matthew 5:44).

Invite the class to write out these teachings, explaining what they think they mean. Is one of these teachings more difficult to put into practice than another? Ask pupils to give reasons for their answers.

You might like to use this as a discussion starter, in order to help pupils think through the choices they make.

Activity

Besides the WWJD wristband, there have been other suggested ways of trying to apply Jesus' teachings to today's world. Some websites have suggested the kind of diet that Jesus would eat, and the choices he would make if he lived in a time when he had to drive a car. Although these ideas might seem bizarre, they could get pupils thinking about religious leaders in a way that helps them develop reasoning about how ideas and beliefs influence behaviour.

Here are some questions that pupils might reflect on:

- What car would Jesus drive and why?
- What would Jesus say to your class and why?
- What television programmes would Jesus watch? What wouldn't he watch?
- What music would Jesus listen to and why?
- How would Jesus vote?
- What would Jesus wear?
- What would Jesus sing?
- What sport might Jesus play and why?

These questions could be controversial: they could encourage disrespect or an inappropriate reaction, so will need careful handling. Pupils could use www.biblegateway.com to search for information to back up their ideas.

This could be a fruitful exercise with the gifted and talented, who might enjoy the lateral nature of this approach.

Cross-curricular links

- English: the importance of stories that teach us about ideas.

Assembly/Reflection

Jesus was an example of a good teacher. What makes a good teacher? What makes a good pupil? How can we make sure that teachers and pupils work well together in the school?

✝

Prayer: the Lord's Prayer

Learning objectives

- All pupils will be able to explain why prayer is important to Christians.
- Most pupils will be able to comment on why the Lord's Prayer is an exemplary prayer.
- Some pupils will be able to comment on the effectiveness of prayer and the themes in the Lord's Prayer.

Starter

Give pupils a version of the Lord's Prayer cut up into sections, and, without reading it to them, ask them to put the prayer back together in the order they think it should be. Do any of the versions radically differ from the original?

Introduction

For Christians, prayer is very important. Prayer is about communication with God. It has two parts to it—talking and listening. Jesus was once asked by his disciples if he could help them to learn to pray. In reply, he gave them an example of a prayer. Some Christians believe that this prayer should be said every day; others see it as an example of how we should pray.

The Lord's Prayer gives four key ideas about how Christians should speak to God:

- Adoration: praising God for who he is.
- Thanksgiving: thanking God for the good things that he has done and will do.

- Confession: saying sorry to God for the bad things that we have done.
- Intercession: asking God for help to change difficult situations or to help people deal with tough times; also, asking God to meet the basic needs we have as people.

According to Matthew's and Luke's Gospels, Jesus gave his disciples a version of the prayer below. In later centuries, other Christians added the words in bold at the end of the prayer, as they felt that it should end with praise to God.

Our Father in heaven,
hallowed be your name.
Your kingdom come,
your will be done,
on earth as it is in heaven.
Give us this day our daily bread,
and forgive us our debts,
as we also have forgiven our debtors.
And lead us not into temptation,
but deliver us from evil.
The kingdom, the power and the glory are yours now and forever.
Amen

 Activity

Divide the class into groups, give each group four lines from the Lord's Prayer, then invite them to think of some movements that show the meaning of the words. One person might say the words, but everyone in the group must mime the actions.

 Activity

Invite pupils to retell the prayer in a form that they can more easily access, such as a rap version.

Cross-curricular links

- English/Languages: explore how to communicate in a way that is effective.
- PSHE: talk about how to voice the issues that concern us.
- Drama: work in groups to produce a mime (as above).

Assembly/Reflection

One kind of prayer is thanksgiving—saying thank you to God for the good things we have. What should we be grateful for? Do we need to thank someone for any of the good things we enjoy?

✝

Parables: Jesus the storyteller

Learning objectives

- All pupils will be able to explain what a parable is.
- Most pupils will be able to show how Jesus used parables.
- Some pupils will be able to develop their own parables to show how effective they can be in communicating values and morals through the story form.

Starter

Photocopy the Bible story of the good Samaritan, as printed below (or download from www.barnabasinschools.org.uk/extra-resources/). Cut the story up into strips and then ask the class, working in groups, to rearrange the pieces into the right order. Can they get it in the right order? Do they make mistakes?

An expert in the Law of Moses stood up and asked Jesus a question to see what he would say. 'Teacher,' he asked, 'what must I do to have eternal life?'

Jesus answered, 'What is written in the Scriptures? How do you understand them?'

The man replied, 'The Scriptures say, "Love the Lord your God with all your heart, soul, strength, and mind." They also say, "Love your neighbours as much as you love yourself."'

Jesus said, 'You have given the right answer. If you do this, you will have eternal life.'

But the man wanted to show that he knew what he was talking about. So he asked Jesus, 'Who are my neighbours?'

Jesus replied: 'As a man was going down from Jerusalem to Jericho, robbers attacked him and grabbed everything he had. They beat him up and ran off, leaving him half dead.

A priest happened to be going down the same road. But when he saw the man, he walked by on the other side.

Later a temple helper came to the same place. But when he saw the man who had been beaten up, he also went by on the other side.

A man from Samaria then came travelling along that road. When he saw the man, he felt sorry for him and went over to him. He treated his wounds with olive oil and wine and bandaged them.

Then he put him on his own donkey and took him to an inn, where he took care of him.

The next morning he gave the innkeeper two silver coins and said, "Please take care of the man. If you spend more than this on him, I will pay you when I return."'

Then Jesus asked, 'Which one of these three people was a real neighbour to the man who was beaten up by robbers?'

The teacher answered, 'The one who showed pity.'

Jesus said, 'Go and do the same!'
LUKE 10:25–37

Introduction

Stories can be very powerful in teaching us ideas, moving us and challenging us to look at the world in new ways. Often, they contain truths about the way we are, which are sometimes difficult to take but are important nevertheless. Jesus used the parable story form to particular effect. His parable about the good Samaritan (printed out for the 'Starter' activity) is a good example.

 Activity

Plot the key parts of the story on the X axis of a graph:

- The man travels down the road.
- The man is attacked by robbers.
- A priest sees the man.
- The priest walks away from the man.
- A temple helper sees the man.
- The temple helper walks away from the man.
- A Samaritan helps the man.
- The Samaritan takes the man to an inn, where he receives more help.

Ask the class to plot the man's emotions on the Y axis of the graph. Taking each key part of the story in turn, if they think that the man has a good emotion about what happens to him, draw a line going up the Y axis. If they think he has a negative emotion, draw the line going down.

The graph can then be used to help pupils produce a piece of writing based on the story, from the point of view of the man who was attacked, in order to help them think about the emotions involved. They could do it also as a poem or a rap, working with others.

⊕ **Activity**

Invite pupils to look at these statements and choose between the parts of the sentence printed in bold. Ask them to give reasons for their choices.

- The man on the road **deserved/did not deserve** to be beaten up.
- The priest was **cowardly/cruel** to ignore the man who had been beaten up.
- The Levite was **cowardly/cruel** to ignore the man who had been beaten up.
- The Samaritan was **brave/foolish** to help the man who had been beaten up.

⊕ **Activity**

Imagine interviewing the key players in the parable for a local news programme. What do they want to say about the way they behaved? Ask pupils to work together to script and film the interview, then play back the results.

⊕ **Activity**

Ask pupils to write a modern parable—a story that tries to explain a moral point (for example, it is wrong to be selfish; we should listen to others; we should avoid racism). They should give the story a realistic setting with believable characters, and make sure that their point is well explained.

Pupils can use a computer to help them or, if they prefer, produce a storyboard. Below are some sentence stems to help them if they choose the storyboard method.

- My parable is set in…
- The first thing that happened in my parable was…
- The next thing that happened was…
- Then…
- The meaning of this parable is that…

⊕ Activity

Another way to tell the parable is shown below. Read the story to the class and ask them to mime each part. Then give them envelopes containing the story cut into strips. (This version of the story can also be downloaded from www.barnabasinschools.org.uk/extra-resources/.) Ask them to arrange the strips into the right order (as they did for the Starter activity) and stick them on to a piece of paper, perhaps with a drawing to accompany each section.

A man was going from Jerusalem to Jericho. This was a difficult journey. The road was all downhill—in fact, it dropped over a thousand feet between the two towns. There were many rocks and hiding places for robbers on the road.

As it was getting dark, some robbers stopped the man and pushed him off his donkey. They attacked him and left him for dead, taking all the money and possessions he had.

A few hours later, a priest came by. He looked over to where the injured man was but decided that it was not safe to stop. Perhaps the robbers would attack him. So he walked by on the other side.

Time passed. A Levite, a religious leader in the temple, was travelling down the road. He heard the groans of the injured man and went over to have a look. He then walked by on the other side.

The injured man thought that he would die.

More time passed. Then another person came down the road. It was a Samaritan man, riding on a donkey. The injured man was very frightened. He was a Jew, and the Samaritans were enemies of the Jews. The injured man thought that the Samaritan would hurt him even more or kill him.

The Samaritan stopped and got off his donkey. From the bag on the donkey's back, he took a container of water and some strips of cloth. He went to the man. He washed the wounds on the injured man's body and bandaged them with the cloth.

The Samaritan then put the injured man on the donkey and walked alongside. Soon they came to an inn. The Samaritan paid for the man to stay there until he had recovered from his wounds.

Jesus told this story to show that, sometimes, unexpected people can do good things. He wanted to remind people that we all need to look after each other.

Cross-curricular links

• English: think about the power of stories to change us.

Assembly/Reflection

Many of Jesus' stories are about the importance of learning to forgive others when they make mistakes. How can we make sure that we are people who forgive others?

✝

Miracle stories

Learning objectives

- All pupils will be able to explain what miracles are and why they are important in the story of Jesus.
- Most pupils will be able to give some personal response to the stories.
- Some pupils will be able to give their own detailed personal responses as well as considering alternatives to their own opinion.

Starter

Look at this story and think about the big claim it is making.

Straight away, Jesus made his disciples get into the boat and start back across to Bethsaida. But he stayed until he had sent the crowds away. Then he said goodbye to them and went up on the side of a mountain to pray.

Later that evening he was still there by himself, and the boat was somewhere in the middle of the lake. He could see that the disciples were struggling hard, because they were rowing against the wind. Not long before morning, Jesus came toward them. He was walking on the water and was about to pass the boat.

When the disciples saw Jesus walking on the water, they thought he was a ghost, and they started screaming. All of them saw him and were terrified. But at that same time he said, 'Don't worry! I am Jesus. Don't be afraid.' He then got into the boat with them, and the wind died down. The disciples were completely confused.

MARK 6:45–51

Introduction

There are several ways in which you could explain the story. You could say:

- It was a miracle. It happened in the way described and, somehow, God was involved.
- The story was written as an exaggeration of something that really happened.
- The story did not happen; it was made up to explain that in the storms of life, Jesus is there, bringing healing and peace.

Which explanation does the class think is the most likely? Which is the least likely? Ask pupils to give reasons for their answers.

The dictionary says that a miracle is 'an event caused by a supernatural agency'. Many people believe that all claims to miracles are wrong, as these things simply do not happen. Others say that miracles are important to show us that Jesus was special, that he was from God.

The Gospel stories feature many different types of miracle:

- Healing miracles, where someone recovers from a physical disease.
- Exorcism, where an evil spirit is removed from a person.
- Feeding miracles, where large numbers of people are fed with very little food.
- Nature miracles, where nature is controlled, as in the stilling of the storm or Jesus walking on the water.
- Resurrection, where a person is brought back from the dead.

Can the class think of any other types?

Activity

Ask pupils to write and draw a miracle story that is supposed to have happened today. They might want to make the miracle have a meaning that is important to everyone. In this story, they should:

- Explain what the miracle was.
- Say whether a god or gods or a special person performed the miracle.
- Give two different reactions to the miracle—one believing and the other not believing what happened.

The miracle story should include some labelled drawings or diagrams. Pupils can use a computer or, if they prefer, they can produce a storyboard. Below are some sentence stems to help them get going with a storyboard.

- The miracle was…
- The miracle was performed by…
- Some people believed this miracle because…
- Some people did not believe this miracle because…
- If I had been there when this miracle was claimed to have happened, I would have thought…

 Activity

The haiku form is a type of poetry that is divided into three lines, with a certain number of syllables in each line. The first line has five, the second has seven and the third has five. Ask pupils to work with a partner to write a haiku capturing the disciples' feelings about Jesus walking on the water.

Activity

One way to help pupils remember something new is to link it with something familiar. Take the weather forecast. Most pupils will have seen one and will be familiar with the pattern of the way it is done. Ask them to work in groups, using a weather forecast technique in order to retell a miracle. By logging on to BBC iPlayer, you can watch a weather forecast in order to remind pupils of how it sounds.

 Activity

Consider the reactions to the miracles of Jesus in the stories themselves:

- Some people believed that the miracles happened and that they showed that Jesus was from God.
- Others believed that Jesus did miracles because an evil power was helping him.
- Others did not believe that the event was a miracle: it was either a con trick or some kind of magic.

Using www.biblegateway.com to find information about miracle stories, imagine working on a magazine called *Miracles Today*, covering the miracles of Jesus. Provide A3 sheets of paper and ask pupils to produce a detailed account of several miracles of Jesus for this magazine. They should write as if they were journalists covering the events, using pictures, headlines and titles to tell the story. They should include several different responses to the miracles.

Cross-curricular links

- History: study the idea of evidence and how things can be proved.
- Science: research the laws of nature and how they work.
- English: consider stories as metaphors for beliefs.

Assembly/Reflection

There are many ways to understand what Jesus' miracles were about. One key idea is that they were all motivated by his desire to help others. What could we do to help others this week?

✝

The last week of Jesus' life

Learning objectives

- All pupils will be able to identify the key events of the last week of Jesus' life.
- Most pupils will be able to comment on the meaning of these events.
- Some pupils will be able to comment on how these events affect Christian behaviour.

Starter

Try to think of a day or a time that is particularly important. Why is it so important?

Introduction

In the Gospels, a great deal of space is devoted to telling us the story of the last week of Jesus' life—a quarter of Matthew's Gospel, five out of 16 chapters in Mark, five out of 24 in Luke and nine out of 21 in John. If you compare that with a biography of Winston Churchill, you will be very surprised: his last days normally occupy only a few paragraphs. For the writers of the Gospels, it was the last few days that really showed who Jesus was and what he was trying to do.

Here is the timeline:

- Sunday: Jesus enters Jerusalem on a donkey and clears the traders from the temple.
- Monday to Wednesday: Jesus visits the temple each day and is asked a series of questions.

- Wednesday: Judas agrees to betray Jesus.
- Thursday evening, 6pm: Jesus and his disciples meet for the Passover meal. Jesus takes the bread and says that it is like his body. He then takes the wine and says that it is like his blood. Jesus tells Judas to leave and do what he must do. He predicts that Peter will deny knowing him three times before the early morning sound of the cockerel.
- Thursday evening, 11pm: Jesus and the disciples go out to the garden of Gethsemane to pray.
- Friday morning, just after midnight: Jesus is arrested on the charge of blasphemy (claiming to be God).
- Friday morning, early hours: Jesus is put on trial before the religious court, the Sanhedrin. False evidence is given. Jesus is tortured. He is then taken to the Roman governor, Pontius Pilate. Pilate is told that Jesus is guilty of treason (planning to bring down the government). Pilate tries to get the Jewish ruler Herod Antipas to deal with Jesus, but Jesus is sent back to Pilate.
- Friday morning, about 6am: Jesus is given a crown of thorns and a purple robe by the Roman soldiers. They also whip him 39 times.
- Friday morning, 8am: Pilate tries to release Jesus but the crowd demand his death.
- Friday morning, 9am: Jesus is put on a cross with a criminal on crosses at either side of him.
- Friday afternoon, 3pm: Jesus dies on the cross. The Romans agree that he is dead. Jesus' body is taken down from the cross and given to Joseph of Arimathea, who has come to collect it with three women followers of Jesus. Before the sun goes down, Jesus' body is wrapped in the grave clothes of the time and then placed in Joseph of Arimathea's tomb, which is cut into the side of a hill.

Activity

Choose one event on the timeline and write a poem about what happened, from the point of view of a disciple.

 Activity

Choose six of the events and, using the internet, try to find images connected with the event.

Cross-curricular links

- History: research how we know what happened in the past, looking at how evidence is gathered.

Assembly/Reflection

The last week of Jesus' life was a tough time. Who could we turn to when things get tough for us? Who will help us out? What help can we give to others when they are in a difficult place?

Palm Sunday

Learning objectives

- All pupils will be able to explain the events of Palm Sunday.
- Most pupils will be able to explain why the events of Palm Sunday are key to the story of Jesus' last week.
- Some pupils will be able to explain why this story shows Jesus' beliefs about himself and why the event provoked both positive and negative responses.

Starter

Play the 'only positives' game. Ask the class to sit in a circle and hand around a marker, such as a ball, while you play some music. When the music stops, the person who is holding the ball is to be praised and told only good things about themselves. (If anyone is negative about a person, they are asked to leave the circle and will not receive the praise that others will get.)

An alternative is the spider diagram game. A person's name is written on a piece of paper, in the middle of a diagram of a spider. On the eight legs, people have to write positive things about the person named.

Introduction

Listen to the story of Jesus' arrival in Jerusalem on Palm Sunday:

Jesus and his disciples reached Bethphage and Bethany near the Mount of Olives. When they were getting close to Jerusalem, Jesus sent two of them on ahead. He told them, 'Go into the next village. As soon as you enter it, you will find a young donkey that has never been ridden. Untie the donkey and bring it here. If anyone asks why you are doing that, say, "The Lord needs it and will soon bring it back."'

The disciples left and found the donkey tied near a door that faced the street. While they were untying it, some of the people standing there asked, 'Why are you untying the donkey?' They told them what Jesus had said, and the people let them take it.

The disciples led the donkey to Jesus. They put some of their clothes on its back, and Jesus got on. Many people spread clothes on the road, while others went to cut branches from the fields.

In front of Jesus and behind him, people went along shouting, 'Hooray! God bless the one who comes in the name of the Lord! God bless the coming kingdom of our ancestor David. Hooray for God in heaven above!'

After Jesus had gone to Jerusalem, he went into the temple and looked around at everything. But since it was already late in the day, he went back to Bethany with the twelve disciples.

MARK 11:1–11

Ask the following questions about the story.

- Describe how Jesus came into Jerusalem. Why do you think he chose this way?
- Is there anything in this story that is difficult to take as history?

Here are some further questions that might be raised by the story.

- What makes a person popular?
- What are the risks if you are popular?
- Some people say that crowds are naturally wise, when so many people all support the same cause. What is one problem with this argument?

Activity

Ask the pupils: Have you ever met someone who is famous? How did you behave? If you have not, how do you think that you would behave? Think of a famous person you would like to meet and write a list of five questions that you would like to ask him or her.

 Activity

The people who met Jesus entering Jerusalem on Palm Sunday saw him as a hero. Ask the class: What qualities do you think make a person a hero? Do you think that you have any of these heroic qualities?

Cross-curricular links

* PSHE: talk about peer pressure.
* English: think about the importance of a hero in a story.

Assembly/Reflection

Jesus was very popular at the beginning of his last week, but, as he stood up for the things he believed to be right, that popularity soon disappeared. Are you prepared to do the right thing even if it does not make you popular?

✜

Cleansing the temple: Jesus gets angry

Learning objectives

- All pupils will be able to explain why Jesus got angry about the traders in the temple.
- Most pupils will be able to assess how effective Jesus' loss of temper would have been in addressing the problem he saw.
- Some pupils will be able to comment in depth on the idea of righteous anger.

Starter

Think about what makes us get angry. Do pupils think that they are always right to get angry?

Introduction

Look at this story:

After Jesus and his disciples reached Jerusalem, he went into the temple and began chasing out everyone who was selling and buying. He turned over the tables of the moneychangers and the benches of those who were selling doves. Jesus would not let anyone carry things through the temple. Then he taught the people and said, 'The Scriptures say, "My house should be called a place of worship for all nations." But you have made it a place where robbers hide!'

The chief priests and the teachers of the Law of Moses heard what Jesus said, and they started looking for a way to kill him.

They were afraid of him, because the crowds were completely amazed at his teaching.

MARK 11:15–18

Ask the following questions:

- Why did Jesus get so upset when he went into the temple?
- Why did the religious leaders want to get rid of Jesus?
- Is there anything in this story that is difficult to take as history?

 Activity

Invite the pupils to complete the sentence stems below, choosing between the alternatives where shown.

- Jesus was **right/wrong** to get angry in the temple because…
- Anger is **never/sometimes** right because…
- I believe that it is right to get angry about…
- I believe that it is not right to get angry about…

 Activity

Ask the class to rewrite the story as if they were eyewitnesses on the side of the chief priests. Pupils need to show how their views on what happened would be different from the views of those who followed Jesus.

 Activity

Invite pupils to write a role-play about anger, building on the idea of being righteously angry, as Jesus was in the story of the cleansing of the temple.

Cross-curricular links

- PSHE: talk about the appropriateness of anger.
- History: research times when people have protested against injustice.
- Citizenship: consider the place of protest in society.

Assembly/Reflection

There are good and bad types of anger. How can we know the difference? What happens when we get angry and cannot control ourselves?

✝

The last supper

Learning objectives

- All pupils will be able to explain the importance of the last supper for Christians.
- Most pupils will be able to explain how the Communion service matters to Christians today.
- Some pupils will be able to explain that the last supper and the Communion service are models of how Christians should behave if they want to follow Jesus.

Starter

Food is important for several reasons. Ask the class to write down as many reasons as possible.

Introduction

On the night before he was arrested, Jesus met with his disciples to celebrate the Passover.

The Christian writer and leader Paul told the Corinthian church about the last meal that Jesus had with his disciples and why it mattered. He was writing no more than 20 years after the events mentioned in the Gospels. According to the story, Judas, one of Jesus' disciples, had left the room in order to go and betray him to the authorities.

I have already told you what the Lord Jesus did on the night he was betrayed. And it came from the Lord himself.

He took some bread in his hands. Then after he had given thanks, he broke it and said, 'This is my body, which is given for you. Eat this and remember me.'

After the meal, Jesus took a cup of wine in his hands and said, 'This is my blood, and with it God makes his new agreement with you. Drink this and remember me.'
1 CORINTHIANS 11:23–25

One way to help pupils understand the nature of what you are studying could be to reconstruct the meal. Take a piece of bread and some blackcurrant juice and ask pupils to share them with each other, perhaps trying to do it in silence. How does this make them feel?

 Activity

It has been said that 'there is enough food for everyone's need, but not for everyone's greed'. What do pupils think about this? Do they agree? Ensure that they can give reasons for their answers, showing that they have thought about it from more than one point of view.

 Activity

Look at this picture of a loaf of bread. What words and ideas might be linked with bread?

Write a poem based on the ideas that you have collected about bread, including the ideas about bread in the story of the last supper.

 Activity

Write a story about the idea of being betrayed by someone and how this might make us feel.

 Activity

Design a mind-map to show all the ideas and feelings that might have been going on in the room when Jesus shared the last supper with his disciples.

Cross-curricular links

- Art: research representations of the last supper.
- English: work on poems and stories (as above).
- PSHE: talk about dealing with difficult emotions.

Assembly/Reflection

Jesus knew that Judas would betray him. How do we feel when people let us down? What should we do about these emotions?

+

The trial of Jesus

Learning objectives

- All pupils will be able to explain the importance of the trial of Jesus.
- Most pupils will be able to explain the illegalities of the trial.
- Some pupils will be able to evaluate the behaviour of all the people involved in the trial of Jesus and consider their motivations.

Starter

Ask pupils to think about a time when they were wrongly accused of doing something—not a time when they pretended to be wrongly treated, but when someone really got it wrong—and how it made them feel. How did they react to the other person who gave them a difficult time?

Introduction

There are many people across the world who are denied the right to a fair trial. One organisation that promotes justice worldwide is Amnesty International, which tries to make sure that, if people are put on trial, they are treated fairly.

It isn't just in our own day that people have had unfair trials. When Jesus was put on trial, the courts that tried him broke many laws of the time, which they should have followed to make sure he was treated fairly.

These injustices included the following:

- Jesus was put on trial at night. The law said that all trials should be in daylight: one reason for this was to ensure that the right person was brought to the court. In an age before electric light, this was not always easy to check at night.
- Witness evidence did not always agree, so two witnesses were required, and they had to agree on all the key points. The Gospels say that even this standard was not reached.
- Jesus was hit while on trial. The law said that no prisoner should be attacked at his own trial.
- Jesus was arrested during a key Jewish religious festival called the Passover. There should not have been a trial at this time, as it was a holy day.

The religious authorities did another thing that was not right. When he was arrested, Jesus was charged with blasphemy—that is, speaking against God. However, when they took Jesus to the Roman governor, Pontius Pilate, they said that Jesus was guilty of treason—that is, he wanted to replace Caesar as a political leader. They did this because they knew that the Romans would not put him to death for claiming to be a god, but they would put him to death if they thought that he was trying to bring down the government.

⊕ Activity

Referring to the accounts in Mark 14:53–64 and Luke 23:1–12, write a charge sheet listing the wrong things that Jesus was accused of doing.

⊕ Activity

Copy and complete these sentence stems, choosing between alternatives in the second:

- It was wrong to put Jesus on trial at night because…
- Jesus **did/did not** deserve to go on trial because…

Cross-curricular links

- ICT: examine some of the miscarriages of justice or unfair trials that Amnesty International is campaigning against across the world.

Assembly/Reflection

The world is often very unfair. What can we do to make that less the case?

✝

Good Friday: Jesus' suffering on the cross

Learning objectives

- All pupils will be able to explain why the death of Jesus on the cross is important to Christians.
- Most pupils will be able to explain some of the different views about what happened to Jesus on the cross.
- Some pupils will be able to explain and evaluate their own and other people's ideas about the meaning of Jesus' death on the cross.

Starter

Ask the pupils: What most upsets you about the world we live in? What do you think are the worst ways in which people treat each other?

Introduction

Why do Christians call the day when Jesus died 'Good Friday'? It doesn't seem sensible to call the day he died a good day, does it? However, Christians believe that it was the day on which, by his death on the cross, evil was defeated. Goodness was seen to defeat all the bad things in the world.

Some Christians display crosses that do not include the figure of Jesus. Others make sure that there is a small statue of him on every cross. Why might there be these differences between Christians? It seems very odd to use a symbol of torture and death as a symbol of hope. For Christians, though, Jesus' death on the cross dealt with the effects of sin—the bad things that people do—because Jesus was willing to die.

Many Christians believe that the last words that Jesus said on the cross are very important, as they reveal his role and what he was seeking to do. These sentences (gathered together from across all four Gospels) have been a source of inspiration for artists, musicians and thinkers over the centuries.

Look at the seven last sentences in turn and think about their meanings. (These verses are available to download from www. barnabasinschools.org.uk/extra-resources/.)

Jesus said, 'Father, forgive these people! They don't know what they're doing' (Luke 23:34).

Could you or I give forgiveness to people who were putting us to death for no good reason?

Jesus replied, 'I promise that today you will be with me in paradise' (Luke 23:43).

Jesus said this to a robber being crucified next to him, who had asked Jesus to remember him when he got to heaven. Even in the worst situation, there is a second chance for a bad person.

When Jesus saw his mother and his favourite disciple with her, he said to his mother, 'This man is now your son.' Then he said to the disciple, 'She is now your mother' (John 19:26–27).

Jesus was not just concerned about himself: he also cared for his mother and his best friend. He knew that, when he died, they would need to support each other through the difficult times they would face.

About three o'clock Jesus shouted, 'Eli, Eli, lema sabachthani?' which means, 'My God, my God, why have you deserted me?' (Matthew 27:46; Mark 15:34).

Jesus is quoting from one of the Psalms in the Old Testament (Psalm 22:1). Many people think he was saying that, whatever he was trying to do by dying on the cross, it had failed. However, Psalm 22 ends in a positive way, so most Bible scholars think he was trying to say that, despite this dark time, good was going to triumph.

Jesus knew that he had now finished his work. And in order to make the Scriptures come true, he said, 'I am thirsty!' (John 19:28).

Jesus would have been physically thirsty, but this verse is also saying that he was keen to make sure that he achieved the purpose of his work.

Jesus said, 'It is finished!' (John 19:30, NIV).

The original Greek word in the text means, 'It is paid in full.' Many Christians would say that this means that the great barrier of sin between God and human beings has been taken down by Jesus' death on the cross.

Jesus shouted, 'Father, I put myself in your hands!' Then he died (Luke 23:46).

These words show Jesus' actions as fulfilling what his Father God wanted.

 Activity

Ask the pupils to choose one of the sentences that Jesus said on the cross and design a picture to illustrate it. They could write the words inside a cross shape and then, around the edge, add some key ideas that are linked with the sentence they have chosen.

⊕ Activity

Ask the class to copy and complete these sentence stems, choosing between alternatives in the last:

- Jesus' death on the cross is important to Christians because…
- The seven last sentences that Jesus said on the cross are important because…
- I think the cross **is/is not** a good symbol for the Christian faith because…

⊕ Activity

Trailers have to be designed with great care to make us want to see a film. In under 30 seconds, they might seek to tell us a little bit about the plot, show parts of the most important scenes and give us some clues about the characters involved.

Using an interactive whiteboard, show pupils a good example of a trailer that makes the case for seeing a particular film. You could select from the trailers you find on www.lovefilm.com.

Divide the class into groups of four or five and ask each group to create and act out a trailer that is relevant to the story of the cross. Groups should try to make these trailers realistic and reflective of the subject, but should also make sure that they are inviting.

This is a good opportunity for peer assessment, where groups analyse the strengths and weaknesses of other groups, perhaps especially considering the following factors:

- Accuracy in relation to the story/quotation being used.
- How clearly the key religious ideas were communicated in the time available.
- Appropriateness of the content.
- Whether the trailer was inviting enough to encourage people to go and see the film.

Cross-curricular links

- Art: look at representations of the cross.
- Media studies: research the production of a film trailer.

Assembly/Reflection

For Christians, Jesus' death on the cross was a selfless act of love. What makes us selfish and how can we stop ourselves being selfish?

✝

Easter Day: the claim of the resurrection

Learning objectives

- All pupils will be able to explain the key story of the resurrection of Jesus.
- Most pupils will be able to explain why belief in the resurrection affects a Christian's beliefs about life after death.
- Some pupils will be able to evaluate the resurrection claim of Christianity, being able to assess whether or not they think the resurrection happened, and, if they think it did not, to develop an alternative understanding of the events.

Starter

Which of the following ideas do pupils believe in?

In just one sentence for each, ask them what they believe and encourage them to give a reason for their beliefs.

- Heaven: a perfect place where God lives and where suffering and evil no longer exist.
- Hell: a place where the wicked are punished for their evil.
- Purgatory: a holding place, where the mixture of good and bad in people is sorted out, getting people ready for heaven.
- Life after death: the idea that a person's soul survives death.
- The resurrection of Jesus: the claim that Jesus came back from the dead.
- Ghosts: the idea that a person can remain on earth in some way after death.
- Death is the end: this life is all there is.

Introduction

Jesus had died. All the disciples knew that, but then, on the Sunday morning, some of the women who had followed him came back from the tomb and told the other disciples that the tomb was empty and they had seen Jesus alive. Even the disciples found this difficult to believe.

The biggest miracle claimed by Christians is that Jesus came back from the dead three days after being killed on the cross, but what actually happened and is there any way of working out the meaning of the story historically? Look at the story and the information that the Gospels give us, and think about what might have happened.

Imagine you were going to prepare a case for the court about what happened, and take a look at some of the evidence. Begin with the evidence from the guards who were told to watch over Jesus' body.

While the women were on their way, some soldiers who had been guarding the tomb went into the city. They told the chief priests everything that had happened. So the chief priests met with the leaders and decided to bribe the soldiers with a lot of money. They said to the soldiers, 'Tell everyone that Jesus' disciples came during the night and stole his body while you were asleep. If the governor hears about this, we will talk to him. You won't have anything to worry about.' The soldiers took the money and did what they were told. Some of the Jewish people still tell each other this story.

MATTHEW 28:11–15

Now, consider what Joseph of Arimathea might have given as his evidence in court.

There was a man named Joseph, who was from Arimathea in Judea. Joseph was a good and honest man, and he was eager for

God's kingdom to come. He was also a member of the Jewish council, but he did not agree with what they had decided.

Joseph went to Pilate and asked for Jesus' body. He took the body down from the cross and wrapped it in fine cloth. Then he put it in a tomb that had been cut out of solid rock and had never been used. It was Friday, and the Sabbath was about to begin.

The women who had come with Jesus from Galilee followed Joseph and watched how Jesus' body was placed in the tomb. Then they went to prepare some sweet-smelling spices for his burial. But on the Sabbath they rested, as the Law of Moses commands.

LUKE 23:50–56

Finally, there is the evidence of the disciples and the women who claimed to have discovered the empty tomb.

Very early on Sunday morning the women went to the tomb, carrying the spices that they had prepared. When they found the stone rolled away from the entrance, they went in. But they did not find the body of the Lord Jesus, and they did not know what to think.

Suddenly two men in shining white clothes stood beside them. The women were afraid and bowed to the ground. But the men said, 'Why are you looking in the place of the dead for someone who is alive? Jesus isn't here! He has been raised from death. Remember that while he was still in Galilee, he told you, 'The Son of Man will be handed over to sinners who will nail him to a cross. But three days later he will rise to life.' Then they remembered what Jesus had said.

Mary Magdalene, Joanna, Mary the mother of James, and some other women were the ones who had gone to the tomb. When they returned, they told the eleven apostles and the others what had happened. The apostles thought it was all nonsense, and they would not believe.

But Peter ran to the tomb. And when he stooped down and looked in, he saw only the burial clothes. Then he returned, wondering what had happened.

LUKE 24:1–12

Over to you…

- What do you make of these witnesses?
- Which do you think are telling the truth?
- Can we trust any of them?
- Can we trust what the Gospel writers were telling us?

A letter from Thomas

Even Jesus' disciples found it difficult to believe that he had risen from the dead. Here is a reading that you could use in your assembly or to help a class to think about the events of the story. This version of the story of Thomas is told as if the disciple himself were writing to a friend about what had happened.

Dear Simon, I cannot begin to tell you about what has happened here in the last week. I may have been a follower of Jesus for three years, but I never imagined that things would turn out the way they have. On Sunday last week, we were all gathered at the top of the hill outside Jerusalem—the Mount of Olives. Jesus had chosen to ride a donkey into town. This seemed really odd to me, but someone who knows the scriptures better than I do said this showed that he was a humble person and yet still a king.

Well, there we all were, and, when the crowd knew that he was coming, they cut down palm branches and threw their coats in front of the donkey as a mark of respect. They expected something great to happen.

Jesus always is full of surprises, so, rather than having a great big rally with all his supporters, do you know what he did? He went into the temple and started attacking the people he thought were ripping off the poor. He has never been able to stand injustice, and, when it comes with a religious look to it, he particularly hates it. Liars and hypocrites have always upset him most.

Then he spent days answering questions that the authorities posed, to try to trap him. All the while, they were planning to have Jesus arrested. We had celebrated the Passover meal and then we had gone to the garden to pray, but they came there, with Judas, to take him away. Within twelve hours, he was hanging on a cross and dying. I went and hid, afraid someone might know that I was one of his followers. I was not proud of myself, I can tell you, but I did not have the courage to do what I knew I ought to do.

Then, a few days ago, most of Jesus' friends were together, but I was away. When I joined them again, they said that Jesus had risen from the dead—and that he had appeared to many people. Well, I have seen grief-stricken people before, and I thought they were just seeing what they wanted to see, so I didn't believe them.

Then I saw him and I knew. It was Jesus. I had said that I would not believe unless I could touch him, but when I saw, I believed.

⊕ Activity

Invite the class to think about these key questions:

- One idea about what happened to the body of Jesus is...
- I think that this...

- Another idea about what happened to the body of Jesus is...
- I think that this...

- Christians think that the resurrection of Jesus is important because...
- I think that the resurrection...

- Science would say about the resurrection...
- I think that this...

Cross-curricular links

- PSHE: talk about coping with loss and dealing with unexpected events.

Assembly/Reflection

The resurrection is about the idea of finding hope when things seem terrible. What is hope? How can we make it part of our daily life? Examine the idea of heaven as a perfect place and how we might be able to improve the world to make it a better place.

Pentecost: the Spirit comes

Learning objectives

* All pupils will be able to explain the importance of Pentecost as the time at which Christians believe the Holy Spirit was given to them.
* Most pupils will be able to explain how the Church grew as a result of the events of Pentecost.
* Some pupils will be able to reflect on how the Church claims to be a supernatural organisation and make a case for or against this belief.

Starter

Many people are afraid of something. Invite pupils to write or draw a list of things that might make people afraid.

Introduction

An important story about the beginning of the Church is the story of what happened at Pentecost.

On the day of Pentecost all the Lord's followers were together in one place. Suddenly there was a noise from heaven like the sound of a mighty wind! It filled the house where they were meeting. Then they saw what looked like fiery tongues moving in all directions, and a tongue came and settled on each person there. The Holy Spirit took control of everyone, and they began speaking whatever languages the Spirit let them speak.

Many religious Jews from every country in the world were living in Jerusalem. And when they heard this noise, a crowd gathered. But they were surprised, because they were hearing everything in their own languages. They were excited and amazed, and said:

'Don't all these who are speaking come from Galilee? Then why do we hear them speaking our very own languages? Some of us are from Parthia, Media, and Elam. Others are from Mesopotamia, Judea, Cappadocia, Pontus, Asia, Phrygia, Pamphylia, Egypt, parts of Libya near Cyrene, Rome, Crete, and Arabia. Some of us were born Jews, and others of us have chosen to be Jews. Yet we all hear them using our own languages to tell the wonderful things God has done.'

Everyone was excited and confused. Some of them even kept asking each other, 'What does all this mean?' Others made fun of the Lord's followers and said, 'They are drunk.'

ACTS 2:1–13

This is a key moment in the story of the Church: it seems to change a group of very frightened people into those who want to share their ideas with others across the world.

Pentecost was originally a harvest festival that also celebrated the giving of the Jewish law. For Christians today, Pentecost is important because it recalls the time when the first followers of Jesus received the Holy Spirit, a part of the Trinity.

 Activity

The disciples were able, according to the story, to speak in different languages. As a group, find out the words for 'Hello' in several languages and copy them on to large pieces of paper in different colours. The class could use them to form a wall display.

 Activity

Many Christians describe the events of Pentecost as the birthday of the Church. If you were sending the Church a birthday card, what would you show on the outside? What would the greeting say inside?

Activity

The events of Pentecost changed the disciples from fearful people to those who were brave enough to spread their message. Ask the class to look at the following list of fears and their meanings, then make a poster to illustrate them. Think about how you could help people deal with these fears.

- Hypnophobia: the fear of being asleep
- Brontophobia: the fear of thunder
- Ophidiophobia: the fear of snakes
- Botanophobia: the fear of plants
- Cardiophobia: the fear of the heart
- Eicophobia: the fear of home surroundings
- Eisoptrophobia: the fear of mirrors or of seeing oneself in a mirror

 Activity

Write a poem to encourage people to be brave in a difficult situation.

Cross-curricular links

- PSHE: talk about overcoming fear.

Assembly/Reflection

Fear is a big part of many people's lives. What fears shape us? When might it be right to be afraid and when might it be wrong?

✝

Paul: from enemy to friend

Learning objectives

- All pupils will be able to explain the importance of Paul to the development of Christianity.
- Most pupils will be able to show how his writings were important in helping to develop the Church.
- Some pupils will be able to comment on whether they think Jesus or Paul was the true founder of the Christian religion and to give detailed reasons for their beliefs.

Starter

Ask pupils to write down three sentences to show what they think the word 'love' means.

- Love is…
- Love is…
- Love is…

Introduction

Paul had an unusual journey to becoming a Christian. He had been called Saul and had been committed to destroying Christians. We know that he was at the execution of one of Jesus' first followers, Stephen, and approved of the killing at the time. He became involved with people trying to arrest and kill Christians. He had heard that a group of Christians were living in the city of Damascus and, on the way there to arrest them, he had a vision of Jesus. This vision told him to stop persecuting Christians and to become one of Jesus' followers himself.

Activity

Worksheet on Paul

This worksheet is available to download from:
www.barnabasinschools.org.uk/ extra-resources/

1. Use the words below to help you complete this sheet.

a. Paul is sometimes described as an _ _ _ _ _ _ _ even though he was not one of the original _ _ _ _ _ _ _ _ _ _ _ _ _ _ _ .

b. Paul was originally called _ _ _ _ . He was _ _ _ _ _ _ and a _ _ _ _ _ citizen.

c. Paul is known to have been present at the death of _ _ _ _ _ _ _ _ , the first Christian _ _ _ _ _ _ .

MARTYR   STEPHEN   SAUL   JEWISH   ROMAN   TWELVE DISCIPLES
APOSTLE

2. Match each word with the right definition.

Persecute ....The experience of a sudden change of belief
Conversion ......To pick on a person or group
Gentile.............A letter (such as those that Paul sent to the churches he worked with)
Epistle ....A non-Jewish person

⊕ Activity

Take a look at the different images of Paul that can be found at www.textweek.com/art/saint_paul.htm. What can we learn about Christian beliefs about Paul from looking at these images?

⊕ Activity

Paul wrote many letters to the early churches to help them understand what was important in their faith. In one of his most famous writings, he tells the Christians in a city called Corinth what love should be about and what it is not.

What if I could speak
all languages of humans
and of angels?
If I did not love others,
I would be nothing more
than a noisy gong
or a clanging cymbal.
What if I could prophesy
and understand all secrets
and all knowledge?
And what if I had faith
that moved mountains?
I would be nothing,
unless I loved others.
What if I gave away all
that I owned
and let myself
be burned alive?
I would gain nothing,
unless I loved others.

Love is kind and patient,
never jealous, boastful,
proud, or rude.
Love isn't selfish
or quick-tempered.
It doesn't keep a record
of wrongs that others do.
Love rejoices in the truth,
but not in evil.
Love is always supportive,
loyal, hopeful,
and trusting.
Love never fails!
1 CORINTHIANS 13:1–8

- Why do you think that this passage is read out at weddings?
- Why do you think that some Christians read this passage at a person's funeral?
- What do you like about this passage? What do you dislike about it?
- How might you change it if you were rewriting it?

Cross-curricular links

- English: study texts and their meanings.
- PSHE: think about the possibility of personal change.

Assembly/Reflection

Think about the qualities of love that Paul mentions in 1 Corinthians 13. How many of these are true in your life? What could you do to make the others part of your life?

+

Worship

Learning objectives

- All pupils will be able to explain what Christians mean by the word 'worship'.
- Most pupils will be able to give examples of different types of Christian worship.
- Some pupils will be able to compare and contrast Christian worship with other religious expressions.

Starter

Say to the pupils, 'Think about an object that is extremely important to you. It might be in your bedroom at home. What does it mean to you and why is it so important?' Ask them to write and draw about this object.

Introduction

'Worship' comes from the words 'worth ship' and refers to something that is worth respecting or of great value. Anything that we think has great value could be an object for worship—for example, a favourite possession or a favourite person. Christians use many different ways to worship God. These can include:

- Prayer (in church, alone or with small groups of believers)
- Reading the Bible (in church, with others or by themselves)
- Singing hymns and other religious songs
- Lighting a candle
- Going on a pilgrimage to a holy place
- Silence: trying to listen to God rather than speaking about their needs

- Attending a major Christian event
- Taking Communion
- Listening to a sermon (a special talk about faith, given during a church service)
- Looking at an icon

There are many other ways to worship. Some people in the Christian church have become involved in setting up groups that meet in coffee shops or in pubs rather than in traditional religious buildings. There have even been attempts to set up a virtual church on the web.

Ask the class to think about these questions and give reasons for their answers:

- Is worship best with others or by yourself?
- Is one way of worship better than others?
- Do all people worship something or not?

One type of worship: icons

For most pupils, the word 'icon' will mean an image on a computer screen, that you click to get information. Explain that an icon is also a religious picture—something that has been a powerful tool for spiritual development in the Orthodox Christian tradition especially. Icons are important images to help explain key ideas of faith; they are objects that help people in their worship and prayer to God. They are not to be worshipped themselves, but act like windows, helping the believer to see into the reality of their faith.

 Activity

Look at icons associated with key areas of the Christian story, such as:

- The madonna and child
- The cross

- The resurrection
- Old Testament stories: for example, the story of the three visitors welcomed by Abraham and Sarah has been used to depict the Trinity

Icons can be found on the website www.econcept.dk/icon/dox.html. Pupils may do their own internet search to find many more.

Challenge pupils to think about the ideas that the icons represent and ask them to find out about the artwork involved. Whereas individuality is valued in many forms of art, icon makers value uniformity, maintaining the same style in their pictures across the centuries. Class members could collect a series of postcards showing these kinds of images; they are also increasingly used on Christmas cards.

Some believers find icons helpful, while others have a deep revulsion for them. Can the pupils suggest why this might be? What is the difference between an icon and an idol? Is it just a matter of attitude?

Some artists have created icons of figures like Gandhi and Martin Luther King, seeing them as saints. You could invite the class to create icons to represent people from the last 100 years.

Cross-curricular links

- Art: study the making of icons and their meaning.

Assembly/Reflection

As we have seen, 'worship' comes from the words 'worth ship'. What is the most important thing or person in your life and why? Should something else be more important?

✣

The Church: being part of God's family

Learning objectives

- All pupils will be able to explain why churches are important to many Christians.
- Most pupils will be able to give detailed examples of how churches help believers.
- Some pupils will be able to think about some of the disadvantages of belonging to an organisation such as the church.

Starter

Ask, 'What are the best things about being in a family? What are the worst things about being in a family?'

Introduction

From the very beginning, being part of a larger group of believers has been important to Christians. Paul wrote that to be a follower of Christ is like being part of a body: we need each other, like a hand needs a foot and like a heart needs the lungs.

The body of Christ has many different parts, just as any other body does. Some of us are Jews, and others are Gentiles. Some of us are slaves, and others are free. But God's Spirit baptised each of us and made us part of the body of Christ. Now we each drink from that same Spirit.

Our bodies don't have just one part. They have many parts. Suppose a foot says, 'I'm not a hand, and so I'm not part of the body.' Wouldn't the foot still belong to the body? Or suppose

an ear says, 'I'm not an eye, and so I'm not part of the body.' Wouldn't the ear still belong to the body? If our bodies were only an eye, we couldn't hear a thing. And if they were only an ear, we couldn't smell a thing. But God has put all parts of our body together in the way that he decided is best.
1 CORINTHIANS 12:12–18

Ask pupils to think about this statement: 'Church is not about the building but about the people.' What does it mean? Do they agree? Encourage them to give reasons for their answers, showing that they have thought about the statement from more than one point of view.

Visiting churches and cathedrals

Try to develop good relationships with local churches so that you can visit them with your pupils, as this helps them to see how faith connects with their local area.

It is important that pupils understand the significance of the major centres of worship, such as cathedrals. Cathedrals are well geared to welcoming pupil groups, although sometimes they may focus on talking about the past rather than about the life of the cathedral as a place of worship today. Try to go to a cathedral where your pupils can experience some form of worship. Hearing or watching worship in its normal context is important to help them develop their understanding of the Christian faith.

Westminster Abbey has a specially built facility for visits. Ask for details from the Chapter House, Westminster Abbey, 20 Dean's Yard, London SW1P 3PA (Tel: 020 7222 5162).

St Paul's Cathedral, also in London, has an educational centre that provides themed studies. In RE, it offers:

- The cathedral as a place of worship
- The Bible
- Signs and symbols
- Spirituality

- The life of Jesus
- Moral issues discussion

Westminster Cathedral (the Roman Catholic centre) caters for school visits throughout the year on weekdays, on a pre-booked basis. Because of the daily Mass schedules, afternoon tours are preferred.

Your local diocesan cathedrals will be happy to give you tours of their buildings. If pupils are unable to visit, the websites of many cathedrals have an impressive amount of material that will explain a great deal more about their importance.

 Activity

The design of a church can express important ideas for Christians. One of the most popular designs is the shape of a cross, which shows how important the death of Jesus is to Christians.

In the last 40 years, many new churches have been built in a circular shape, to show that everyone has equal access to God and that all can be blessed.

Ask pupils to look at the illustrations below.

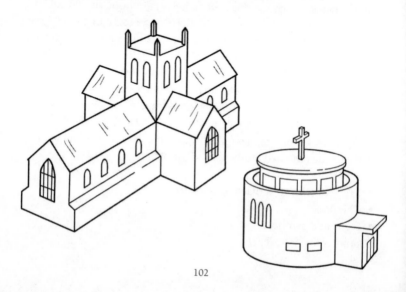

Using this information and their own imagination, they should design a three-dimensional church for the 21st century. They can then try to make it out of cardboard boxes and other modelling 'junk'. Should it be cross-shaped or circular? Should it be a different shape, to help people concentrate on another key part of their faith?

 Activity

Ask the pupils to design a poster to explain, from a Christian point of view, why it is important to go to church. They can use a computer to help them if they wish. The target audience will be children who are not normally attracted to church. Perhaps, by highlighting Jesus in a new and exciting way, the poster design might get their attention.

The posters must use colour and can include drawings, lettering and symbols from the internet as well as the pupils' own original ideas.

Cross-curricular links

- Design and Technology: research the building of a church.
- History: study the influence of the church on society.

Assembly/Reflection

Reflect on the idea that the church is like a body. Consider how, in every community, every person is special and can add something. You could relate this idea to a school event, such as sports day or a drama production, to show that a willingness to take part and join fully in community activities helps the whole community to become stronger.

✛

The Church: expressing faith

Learning objectives

- All pupils will be able to explain that churches have different ways of expressing their faith.
- Most pupils will be able to give examples of these differences in practice.
- Some pupils will be able to comment on the ways they think faith could be expressed today.

Starter

Ask pupils to make a list of activities or stories that they like, then compare lists with a person sitting nearby. What is similar on their lists? What is different?

Introduction

There are many different ways of expressing faith in the Christian church. Just like the lists that the pupils compiled and shared with classmates, there are things that these expressions have in common and there are differences between them. Different types of church were started at different times in history, to stress aspects of faith that were particularly important to them. Other churches might disagree with these aspects of faith or might see them as not so important.

For example, for a Roman Catholic Christian, there is an emphasis on including paintings and statues in churches. Some other Christians do not like to include so many images in their churches.

Labyrinths

The tradition of making labyrinths or mazes is an ancient one. The idea comes from Greek mythology, in which a labyrinth was built on the island of Crete to house the minotaur (half-man, half-bull), eventually killed by the hero Theseus. Labyrinth designs are now used by the Christian church. There is a famous labyrinth at Chartres Cathedral in France.

In the alternative worship movement in the UK church, many congregations have developed the use of the labyrinth as a way of helping a person to stop and think.

Symbols

Many types of Christian worship can be expressed through symbolic objects, actions and gestures.

Silence

Silence can be rather threatening for people, so this is something you might wish to explore—perhaps by taking pupils to a monastery where there is a rule of silence. How will they cope with it? Alternatively, take them to a Quaker meeting house and ask a member of the community to explain the importance of silence.

One way to remember a tragic accident and the victims or casualties of such an event is with a commemorative moment of silence—for example, to remember events like 9/11 and the tsunami of Boxing Day 2004. Why, in an age that is thought to be less religious than previous times, have these moments of silence become more important? Is it really about silence for its own sake, or is this a roundabout way of acknowledging the need for prayer? Ask pupils to say when they think that silence is appropriate and when it is not.

Sara Maitland's book *A Book of Silence* (Granta, 2008) might be a stimulating introduction to these issues, for teachers.

Activity

Mark out a labyrinth design on the floor using tape or paper. (See www.labyrinth.org.uk for an example of a pattern you could use.) At intervals along the route of the labyrinth, place items that are designed to make a person think. You could use themed objects: for example, around a labyrinth about the Communion, you could place the following:

- A loaf of bread or selection of breads
- A wine glass
- Non-alcoholic grape juice
- An icon of Christ on the cross
- An embroidered hassock
- A lighted candle

Ask pupils to walk around the labyrinth and then stop and think about the items they have seen. Ask them to write down or draw one response to these items. How has walking the labyrinth made them feel? Do they think they understand religion a little better by taking part?

 Activity

Ask pupils to design their own international symbol for worship, perhaps with labels at the side to explain its symbolism or special meaning.

Invite pupils to write down their reasons for choosing to express worship with this symbol. What does it mean? What emotion should it produce?

 Activity

Ask pupils to reflect on the title of a song by Depeche Mode, 'Enjoy the silence'. How can silence be enjoyed? In the words of another song by the Tremeloes, 'Silence is golden'. What might this mean? Ask pupils why they think that Christian believers often keep a moment of silent reflection after the Bible has been read aloud in church.

Cross-curricular links

- Art: design symbols.
- Design and Technology: make a labyrinth (as above).
- Mathematics: study the idea of the labyrinth and finding a solution to a puzzle.

Assembly/Reflection

Why might times of silence be a good idea? Someone once pointed out that we have one mouth but two ears, which suggests that we should be doing twice as much listening as speaking.

✢

Baptism: becoming part of the Church

Learning objectives
- All pupils will be able to explain the importance of baptism.
- Most pupils will be able to explain how baptism is practised differently by different churches.
- Some pupils will be able to give their own personal response to what happens at baptism.

Starter
Ask pupils to write the word 'water' in the middle of a page and try to find as many words or phrases as possible that are associated with it.

Introduction
There are several different views about baptism. Some believers, including Roman Catholics and Anglicans, think that baptism should be open to newly born children, as a way of welcoming them into the Christian faith. The baptism of infants is also called 'christening'. (Some churches, such as the Methodist Church, the United Reformed Church and the Church of England, baptise both adults and infants.)

The Church of England's website (www.churchofengland.org) talks about baptism in this way:

In baptism, you as parents are: thanking God for his gift of life, making a decision to start your child on the journey of faith and asking for the Church's support.

For your child, baptism marks the start of a journey of faith, which involves turning away from all that is evil, turning towards Christ and becoming a member of the local and worldwide Christian family.

Baptism is a very important time in the life of a family as it shows the commitment they are making to the child. The parents will also appoint friends or other family members as godparents, to care for the spiritual life of the child. Godparents promise to support the child with their prayers and by their example.

Does being baptised automatically make a person a Christian? Christians can disagree with each other about this question. Baptist Christians, for example, believe that only people old enough to make up their own minds should be baptised. The Baptist Union's website (www.baptist.org.uk) says:

A baptism in a Baptist church is nearly always by full immersion. A Baptist church often has a baptismal pool at the front of the church that is usually hidden under the floor, with steps going down into it...

At the service itself, any [person] being baptised will often [explain] how they became a Christian and why they have chosen to be baptised. Then, immediately before baptism, they will be asked basic questions of commitment...

A minister normally baptises. He or she will hold the person being baptised, placing one hand on their back and the other on their chest. They will say the words, 'I baptise you in the name of the Father, of the Son, and of the Holy Spirit', and plunge the person being baptised backwards so that they are fully immersed in the water, before raising them back up to standing position. They then leave the water.

The person baptised will often be welcomed into church membership at Communion in the same service or at the next opportunity.

Look at the images overleaf. Why do you think the font or baptism pool is so important to Christians?

Should parents bring their children to baptism or should people be allowed to wait until they can make up their own mind about it? What does the class think?

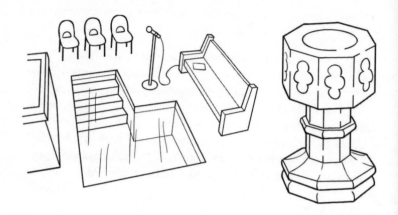

Some people have suggested that there should be a ceremony of de-baptism for people who have been baptised earlier in life but now do not want to belong to a Christian church. What does the class think about this?

Encourage pupils to give reasons for their answers, showing that they have thought about the questions from more than one point of view.

 Activity

Look at some designs for baptism cards online. Ask pupils to design their own card for either a child's christening or a believer's baptism.

Cross-curricular links

- English: write a script for a ceremony of some kind.
- PSHE/Citizenship: talk about belonging to a community.

Assembly/Reflection

Baptism is about having a new start. Can we allow people to make a new start when they have hurt us in some way?

✠

Confirmation: making a choice

Learning objectives

- All pupils will be able to explain why some Christians think confirmation is important.
- Most pupils will be able to unpack the idea of being responsible for our own faith.
- Some pupils will be able to explain how confirmation shows devotion to a faith.

Starter

When can a person be considered an adult? Ask pupils to give reasons for their answers to this question.

Introduction

There should come a point in everyone's life when they become responsible for their own actions. In England, ten-year-olds (not their parents) will be held responsible if they break a law. People can get married with their parents' consent at 16, but have to be 18 before they can vote in an election. Many people feel that we need to choose a single age at which people are considered responsible in these different ways. Others think it is best to keep things as they are, as people may be ready for some responsibilities but not others at a certain age.

In the Jewish religion, boys are considered to be men at the age of 13 and girls are seen as women at the age of 12. They can take a full part in their faith from those ages. However, for those who undertake Christian confirmation, the issue is not about their age but about whether or not they are ready.

The Church of England's website (www.churchofengland.org) talks about confirmation in this way:

Confirmation marks the point in the Christian journey at which you affirm for yourself the faith into which you have been baptised and your intention to live a life of committed discipleship. This affirmation is confirmed through prayer and the laying on of hands by the confirming bishop. The Church also asks God to give you power through the Holy Spirit to enable you to live in the way of Jesus.

One of the most important acts within the service is when the bishop places his hand upon the head of each individual. He traces the sign of the cross with oil on the person's forehead and prays, 'Confirm, O Lord, your servant with your Holy Spirit.' The newly confirmed person responds with the word 'Amen'.

Some denominations that perform believers' baptism do not have a confirmation ceremony. Like confirmation, the baptism service is the rite by which they become full adult members.

 Activity

Some countries hold non-religious ceremonies to welcome a person into adulthood. Ask pupils, working in pairs, to use ICT to create a leaflet showing what such a ceremony might contain. It might, for example, include some promises that might be made by a person claiming to be mature.

Activity

Confirmation

This worksheet is available to download from
www.barnabasinschools.org.uk/extra-resources/.

Use the words below to help you complete this sheet.

Confirmation is important to some _ _ _ _ _ _ _ _ _ _ because it is the service by which they become full adult _ _ _ _ _ _ _ of the Christian Church.

Confirmation is when young people publicly _ _ _ _ _ _ _ the _ _ _ _ made on their behalf during _ _ _ _ _ _ baptism.

Many Christians believe that _ _ _ _ _ _ _ _ _ _ _ _ brings them closer to _ _ _ and improves their relationship with the _ _ _ _ _ _ .

Christians also think that it enables them to receive strength and guidance from the _ _ _ _ _ _ _ _ _ _ . For some Christians, confirmation means that they can now accept _ _ _ _ _ _ _ _ _ _ _ _ _ (bread and wine).

GOD   MEMBERS   CONFIRM   INFANT   VOWS   CHRISTIANS
CONFIRMATION   HOLY SPIRIT   CHURCH   HOLY COMMUNION

Cross-curricular links

- English: write the words for a ceremony (as above).
- PSHE: talk about maturity.
- Citizenship: talk about becoming a responsible citizen.

Assembly/Reflection

Confirmation is about accepting that we are responsible for our actions. How do we know when we are becoming more mature?

✛

Marriage: making a commitment

Learning objectives

- All pupils will be able to explain why marriage is important to Christians.
- Most pupils will be able to describe the key parts of a wedding ceremony that show Christian belief.
- Some pupils will be able to reflect on the practicality of living out Christian ideals about love in the real world.

Starter

Why do people get married? Ask pupils to list the possible reasons, working with a partner.

Introduction

The website www.yourchurchwedding.org (a special Church of England site) talks about marriage in this way:

Marriage is a very ancient idea. The Bible suggests it goes right back to Adam and Eve, who were 'made for each other' (Genesis 2). Jesus' teaching on marriage, as exclusive, unbreakable and forging a new family unit, drew on this original blueprint. And Jesus loved a good wedding: he turned water into wine at a wedding reception (John 2), his first recorded miracle... So marriage has always been part of God's good plan for us... A good marriage is healthy, freeing and life-giving... Christians believe that marriage is a gift from God. There is something in a public commitment of this magnitude that has a spiritual element to it and which can transform a relationship to a new and deeper level.

Activity

Marriage

This worksheet is available to download from www.barnabasinschools.org.uk/extra-resources/.

Use the words below to help you complete this sheet:

Christians believe that marriage is important because it is a gift or _ _ _ _ _ _ _ _ from God.

Christians say that marriage brings two people together to love, help and support each other through life. They believe that, through marriage, they learn about God's _ _ _ _ for human beings.

Christians believe that marriage should be the relationship in which people enjoy sexual intercourse and have _ _ _ _ _ _ _ _.

Every type of church has slightly different ways to _ _ _ _ _ _ _ _ _ marriage. They all contain _ _ _ _ that the couple make to each other in the presence of _ _ _ and the witnesses at the service.

The priest taking the marriage service will ask if there is any _ _ _ _ _ _ why the couple should not be married. If there is no reply, the _ _ _ _ _ _ will declare the couple to be husband and _ _ _ _.

WIFE   PRIEST   REASON   BLESSING   GOD   VOWS   CHILDREN
LOVE   CELEBRATE

⊕ Activity

Invite the pupils to write their own sets of vows or promises that they would be willing to make to another person.

⊕ Activity

Ask the pupils to imagine that they are wedding planners. They should try to plan a wedding ceremony and reception that might please the following types of couples:

- Both are interested in football.
- Both like animals and the countryside.
- Both are keen on history.
- Both like the sea.

Cross-curricular links

- PSHE: explore the idea of promises.
- Art: design a wedding outfit for either bride or groom.
- English: write vows and promises (as above).

Assembly/Reflection

A successful marriage is based on respect, love and trust. These are qualities that we need in all our relationships. How could we develop them in this school?

✣

Funerals: saying goodbye

Learning objectives

- All pupils will be able to explain key ideas connected with a Christian funeral service.
- Most pupils will be able to reflect on how belief influences Christian behaviour.
- Some pupils will be able to consider what is the best way to celebrate someone's life.

Starter

Here are some questions for pupils to think about, with a partner.

- What is the right way to celebrate the life of someone?
- What should you say and what shouldn't you say at a funeral?

Introduction

For Christians, funerals can often be times when they are both sad and happy. They are sad about losing someone, but they can be happy at the idea of a person going to heaven. The idea of heaven is of a perfect place. What could we do to make the world a better place, so that it is closer to being heaven on earth?

On the Church of England's website (www.churchofengland. org), we can read the following:

A funeral is used to mark the end of a person's life here on earth. Family and friends come together to express grief, give thanks for the life lived and commend the person into God's keeping. These can be a small, quiet ceremony or a large occasion in a packed church.

When someone dies it is not an easy time. People feel sad and might feel regret about what they did not say or do before that person died.

Activity

Funerals

This worksheet is available to download from
www.barnabasinschools.org.uk/extra-resources/.

Use the words below to help you complete this sheet.

Christians believe that there is _ _ _ _ after death. They call it _ _ _ _ _ _ _ life.

A Christian _ _ _ _ _ _ _ marks the passing of a believer from this life to eternal life. It also gives people the opportunity to express their feelings and beliefs about death and to say goodbye to someone they have cared about. Traditionally, those who are _ _ _ _ _ _ _ _ the person who has died will wear dark clothing to express their feelings of sadness. An example of this might be to wear a _ _ _ _ _ suit and tie.

Funeral services take place in either a church or a _ _ _ _ _ _ _ _ _ _ _. The service normally consists of hymns, prayers and a talk, called a _ _ _ _ _ _, about death and the Christian hope of life after death.

The ceremony reminds Christians that life is a precious gift from God. In it, they also reflect on Jesus' life and _ _ _ _ _ _ _ _ _ _ _ _. The idea of the resurrection is that Jesus came back to life, after having died. It makes Christian think that they will one day meet their relatives in heaven.

After the funeral service, the body is either cremated or buried in a church graveyard or another consecrated place. The final part of the ceremony is called the _ _ _ _ _ _ _ _ _.

SERMON   FUNERAL   CREMATORIUM   ETERNAL   COMMITTAL
BLACK   RESURRECTION   LIFE   MOURNING

⊕ Activity

An obituary is a summary written about a person after they have died. Ask the pupils to find out about someone from history and try to write his or her life story in the style of an obituary that you might find in a newspaper today.

Cross-curricular links

- English: write an obituary (as above).
- History: research the way death has been treated down the centuries.
- PSHE: talk (sensitively) about death and bereavement.

Assembly/Reflection

When is it right to cry? Why might crying help us to cope with tough times?

✢

Pilgrimages: holy journeys

Learning objectives

- All pupils will be able to explain the idea of pilgrimage within Christianity.
- Most pupils will be able to describe in detail at least one example of a pilgrimage.
- Some pupils will be able to give clear descriptions of at least two pilgrimages as well as giving a detailed response to the question 'How is life like a pilgrimage?'

Starter

Ask pupils to think about a place that is important to them. Why is it important? Did something special happen there?

Introduction

Right from the earliest days of Christianity, pilgrimages were very important. A pilgrimage is a journey to visit a key place where there was an important event. Many Christians wanted to visit Jerusalem in Israel, as it was there that Jesus was put to death and, they believed, rose from the dead. Some also wanted to go north, to the Galilee area. As Christianity developed, other places began to be seen as special. At Lourdes in France, the Virgin Mary was believed to have appeared to a young girl called Bernadette. Now millions of people go there each year in the hope of being healed by a miracle.

Some Christians may not go to specific pilgrimage places, but they attend events that gather people together to worship. One of these events is Spring Harvest, which meets in several different places: members of different churches can worship together there. Another is Greenbelt, an arts festival that has encouraged

Christians to think about the arts as well as to try out new and old ideas to help them in their relationship with God.

Going to see a place where inspirational things are supposed to have happened can help believers to understand more about their faith. They might understand the stories in the Bible better if they can see the places mentioned. The journey to such places might be important in itself, as it gives the travellers time to think about what is really important in their lives.

 Activity

Many hymns use the idea of pilgrimage to explain the journey of the Christian faith and the struggles involved in it. Look at some examples, such as 'To be a pilgrim' by John Bunyan or 'One more step along the world I go' by Sydney Carter. Ask pupils why hymns using the image of a journey might be helpful to people.

Would the class agree that life is like a pilgrimage? Encourage them to give reasons for their answer.

 Activity

Invite the class to find these places of pilgrimage on a map:

- Iona in Scotland
- Rome in Italy
- Lourdes in France
- Jerusalem in Israel

 Activity

Ask the class to design either a poster that shows an important journey they have made or would like to make, or a mind-map explaining the key ideas about the effect that pilgrimage has on a person's beliefs and how these ideas help Christians today. Pupils should use colour to make their designs bright and attractive.

Cross-curricular links

- Geography: study the importance of places and journeys.
- History: research how particular places become important.
- English: read and write stories about journeys.

Assembly/Reflection

Using the hymns by John Bunyan and/or Sydney Carter, help pupils to reflect on their life as a journey and what that might mean.

✣

The Bible: the 'word' of God

Learning objectives

- All pupils will be able to explain why the Bible is important to Christians.
- Most pupils will be able to give their own views on the Bible.
- Some pupils will be able to analyse their own views and the views of others.

Starter

Which stories are the pupils' favourites? Why do they like these stories? Why do most people think that stories are very important?

Introduction

Most Christians see the Bible as being a very special book indeed. They sometimes describe it as the 'word of God'. The Bible explains in its own pages why it is important.

Everything in the Scriptures is God's Word. All of it is useful for teaching and helping people and for correcting them and showing them how to live. The Scriptures train God's servants to do all kinds of good deeds.

2 TIMOTHY 3:16–17

What God has said isn't only alive and active! It is sharper than any double-edged sword. His word can cut through our spirits and souls and through our joints and marrow, until it discovers the desires and thoughts of our hearts.

HEBREWS 4:12

Your word is a lamp that gives light wherever I walk. Your laws are fair and I have given my word to respect them all.

PSALM 119:105–106

What might these quotations teach us about the Bible?

Many Christians talk about the Bible as being like a library of books, not just one book. It is divided into two parts—the Old Testament, containing 39 books, and the New Testament, with 27 books. These books were written over a period of 1000 years. There is a great variety of different types of writing in them.

Red-letter Bibles

In the past few years, different versions of the Bible, using different-coloured print to highlight particular ideas, have become popular. They include the following:

- The words of Christ: these Bibles highlight the words used by or quoted from Jesus.
- The Poverty and Justice Bible: this Bible highlights the texts connected with the care of the poor and the need for social justice.
- The Green Bible: this Bible highlights teachings linked to the care of the environment.

Activity

Ask the pupils to think about whether 'red-letter' Bibles are a good idea or not. Might the red-letter approach distort the whole message of the Bible by making one issue or person seem more important than others, or by giving the impression that the Bible is mainly about one particular issue?

You might want the class to look at one of these types of Bible in detail. What support material is included in the Bible, to justify the highlighting of one particular moral issue?

Would it be possible to have a Peace Bible, given the diversity of views on war that are found in the whole of the Bible?

What other issues might the class want to highlight, which the existing 'red-letter' Bibles don't cover—such as the role of women, racism or drug and alcohol abuse?

Should other religions have editions of their holy books that emphasise particular teachings or would this be misleading?

Cross-curricular links

• English: think about the power of stories to change us.
• Citizenship: consider how moral codes can be reinforced by religion.

Assembly/Reflection

For religious people, the Bible contains a great deal of wisdom. What is the difference between wisdom and knowledge? How can we show that we are people who are developing both?

✛

The Psalms

Learning objectives

- All pupils will be able to explain what a psalm is.
- Most pupils will be able to comment on themes contained in the Psalms.
- Some pupils will be able to write their own version of a psalm.

Starter

Ask the pupils to think of one of their favourite songs and say what appeals to them about it. Why are songs so important in people's lives? Invite the class to draw a spider diagram to show some of the reasons why songs might be important.

Introduction

Think for a moment about how important music and songs are to people. Songs help us to celebrate the good things in life, like falling in love, birthdays or marriage.

We might sing to encourage our team or to cheer ourselves up at a football or rugby match. Singing can sometimes help us to reflect on the important things in life or strengthen us to face difficulties. There are very few people who do not have a favourite song.

Music and words can be enormously powerful in helping us change our mood. We might use a loud song to help us express anger or to celebrate something, or a quieter song when we are feeling lonely or sad.

Right in the middle of the Bible is a collection of songs, poems and prayers that are known as the Psalms. The Psalms were written by a number of different authors, almost certainly including Israel's King David. They were probably used in the worship services in the Jewish temple before it was destroyed in AD70. Today, the Psalms or versions of them are used by Jews in their synagogues and by Christians in their church services.

The Psalms reflect a wide variety of events and emotions. There are psalms about how we feel when friends have betrayed us. Some are about how nations deal with defeat in battle. Many are very personal, describing how the writer is feeling towards God.

Some psalms today have become linked with particular events. For example, Psalm 23 is often used at funeral services. Read it through carefully and ask the class to say why they think Christians would want it sung or said at funeral services:

You, Lord, are my shepherd. I will never be in need.
You let me rest in fields of green grass.
You lead me to streams of peaceful water,
and you refresh my life.
You are true to your name,
and you lead me along the right paths.
I may walk through valleys as dark as death,
but I won't be afraid.
You are with me,
and your shepherd's rod makes me feel safe.
You treat me to a feast, while my enemies watch.
You honour me as your guest,
and you fill my cup until it overflows.
Your kindness and love will always be with me
each day of my life,
and I will live for ever in your house, Lord.
PSALM 23

Other psalms form the basis of hymns that are sung in church. The hymn 'All people that on earth do dwell' (based on Psalm 100) is used in the UK at the coronation of a new king or queen. The class might like to reflect on why it is used in this way.

Shout praises to the Lord, everyone on this earth.
Be joyful and sing as you come in to worship the Lord!
You know the Lord is God!
He created us, and we belong to him;
we are his people, the sheep in his pasture.
Be thankful and praise the Lord
as you enter his temple.
The Lord is good!
His love and faithfulness will last for ever.
PSALM 100

Some of the Psalms have influenced the songwriters of today. One of them is Psalm 40.

I patiently waited, Lord, for you to hear my prayer.
You listened and pulled me from a lonely pit
full of mud and mire.
You let me stand on a rock with my feet firm,
and you gave me a new song,
a song of praise to you.
Many will see this, and they will honour
and trust you, the Lord God.
PSALM 40:1–3

Another is Psalm 137. This psalm has had great power to appeal to people who feel weak and crushed. When the king of Babylon invaded Israel in the year 597BC, he forcibly removed some of the Israelites to his country. One of the Israelites recorded his feelings of anger and confusion at what had happened:

Beside the rivers of Babylon we thought about Jerusalem,
and we sat down and cried.
We hung our small harps on the willow trees.
Our enemies had brought us here as their prisoners,
and now they wanted us to sing and entertain them.

They insulted us and shouted, 'Sing about Zion!'
Here in a foreign land,
how can we sing about the Lord?
Jerusalem, if I forget you, let my right hand go limp.
Let my tongue stick to the roof of my mouth,
if I don't think about you above all else.
PSALM 137:1–6

 Activity

Listen to '40' by U2 and 'The rivers of Babylon' by Boney M (both available on iTunes). Ask the pupils why they think writers and musicians are still influenced by the Psalms.

 Activity

Invite the pupils to take one of the psalms featured in this section and write it out neatly, drawing pictures around it to show its themes.

 Activity

Ask the pupils to write a modern-day psalm, following a certain pattern—explaining where a person is, saying why the person might be feeling unhappy or far from God, then saying how they might find meaning in the experience, and hope for the future.

Cross-curricular links

- English: study the power of poetry to change or reflect people's ideas about the world.
- Music: consider the power of songs.
- PSHE: talk about how we deal with feelings of praise and revenge.

Assembly/Reflection

Take one of the psalms, such as Psalm 23, and reflect on its importance in helping people through difficult times.

✢

Living as a Christian today

Learning objectives

- All pupils will be able to explain some of the issues that Christians face as they try to live out their faith in today's world.
- Most pupils will be able to explain Christian responses to issues they face and be able to comment on them from more than one point of view.
- Some pupils will be able to analyse the strengths and weaknesses of some opinions as well as developing their own.

Starter

How hard is it to explain your point of view and to keep to it when other people do not share it? Discuss this question in class.

Introduction

Look at these words of Jesus:

'You are like salt for everyone on earth. But if salt no longer tastes like salt, how can it make food salty? All it is good for is to be thrown out and walked on.

'You are like light for the whole world. A city built on top of a hill cannot be hidden, and no one would light a lamp and put it under a clay pot. A lamp is placed on a lampstand, where it can give light to everyone in the house. Make your light shine, so that others will see the good that you do and will praise your Father in heaven.'

MATTHEW 5:13–16

Why might Jesus have compared his followers to salt and light? Use the internet to find out about the properties of salt.

In an article for *The Guardian* (29 July 2009: see www.guardian.co.uk), the 'Ethical and Green Living' journalist Leo Hickman listed his ten most valuable items, which included pictures by his children. Explain to the class that some of the most valuable things we possess are not necessarily of great monetary value. You might also challenge pupils to consider whether 'possessions' are just material objects or whether they might include personal qualities or intangible things, such as friendship.

Think about the relevance of Jesus' teaching: 'Your heart will always be where your treasure is' (Matthew 6:21).

Many religious believers undertake projects to help the natural world. One example is A Rocha, a Christian-based environmental charity. Their projects are frequently cross-cultural in character and have a community emphasis, with a focus on science and research, practical conservation and environmental education. Their site in Southall, London, is a reclaimed rubbish tip, which A Rocha have transformed into a nature reserve. They have also produced books and information about how to improve the local environment. They are willing to accept visitors and may well be happy to supply a speaker for any themed events.

Activity

Ask the pupils to compile a list, like Leo Hickman's, of the top ten possessions they own.

If you feel that a list of ten is too ambitious for the individuals in your class, you could set this as a paired exercise. You could also collect the answers and work out the top ten items or qualities that dominate the group as a whole.

Challenge the class to decide, if they could only have one thing, what it would be. Rule out the absolute essentials, such as food, water, housing and clothing, so that the pupils can think beyond their immediate needs.

Encourage pupils to try to distinguish between needs and wants.

Activity

Invite the pupils to decorate eggs with images of the world. This is one way to illustrate the fragile nature of the world, which is easy to understand at one level but not at another.

 Activity

Encourage pupils to study the website www.arocha.org and think about its effectiveness in communicating the Christian vision of the environmental charity A Rocha.

Cross-curricular links

- Geography: research various aspects of care for the environment.
- Citizenship: talk about belonging to a group.

Assembly/Reflection

'Be the change that you want to see' (Mahatma Gandhi). How might we make this true in our school community, in our families and in our world?

✝

Further ideas for teachers

You could use the following ideas to help you consolidate the learning that you have been bringing about with your class. Alternatively, use the techniques suggested here as another way to develop the teaching of Christianity.

Noughts and crosses

Give a new spin to this simple game. Divide the class into those who will play for the noughts and those who will be siding with the crosses. Players will score by answering a question and filling in each square. If they fail on their turn, the other team gets the opportunity to fill the square if they get the answer right.

You will need nine questions. Here are some that you could use in connection with the life of Jesus:

- Name the town where Jesus was born. (Bethlehem)
- Name the town where Jesus grew up. (Nazareth)
- In which city was Jesus put to death? (Jerusalem)
- Name the books in the Bible that tell the life story of Jesus. (The Gospels of Matthew, Mark, Luke and John)
- What did Jesus use at a meal to represent his body and blood? (Bread and wine)
- Who betrayed Jesus? (Judas)
- On what day did Jesus die on the cross? (Good Friday)
- On what day did Jesus come back from the dead? (Easter Sunday)
- For how long did Jesus appear to the disciples after his resurrection? (Forty days)

The aim, of course, is to get three noughts or crosses in a row, but, if that cannot be achieved, the winner will be the first team to get five out of nine questions right.

Bookmarks

Give out sheets of A4 paper, each marked with two long rectangles. Ask pupils to fill in the spaces with some key images of the Christian faith. You could then have them laminated for use as bookmarks.

Give us a clue!

In the 1980s, the television programme *Give Us a Clue* featured celebrities playing charades. Why not use charades to explain some key biblical ideas? For example, pupils could mime parables such as the lost son (Luke 15:11–31) or, to be a little more ambitious, stories such as the creation of the world or the resurrection.

In order to set the charades up properly, you might need to think in advance about the actions that introduce them. You could ask one set of pupils to devise a set of appropriate actions that will communicate the intentions successfully.

Divide the class into two or more teams to compete. This might serve as a good plenary activity or, indeed, an informal way of reinforcing what pupils have learnt, at the end of term. It has the advantage of appealing to pupils whose preferred learning style is kinaesthetic.

T-shirts

It has become quite fashionable to advertise all kinds of causes on T-shirts. Religious groups have certainly got in on the act. Faithgear, for example, is a clothing company started by Christians in Southall who use Punjabi script for key Bible words or verses.

T-shirt adverts have to be arresting, containing a limited number of words and an image or logo that grabs the attention.

Ask the pupils to do an internet search for faith-related T-shirts, then set them the challenge of producing their own. This exercise could be connected to a moral issue or could be used to present an idea from a faith in an arresting way. You might ask the class to create their designs first on a T-shirt template on the computer and then as a 3D version.

Although some stores sell plain white T-shirts very cheaply, the shirts are not always ethically sourced. If you buy T-shirts for the class to use, do try to make sure they come from a good source.

Twitter

The idea of Twitter is to send messages of no more than 140 characters. Challenge the class to take an important teaching or event and try to sum it up in 140 characters. For example, you could tweet the birth of Jesus as:

Messiah born. Angels alert shepherds. Wise men visit. Herod kills children. Family to Egypt.

You could ask pupils to work on the following events:

- Palm Sunday
- Good Friday
- The Christian idea of the Trinity
- The message of the Bible

Is it easier to summarise incidents or ideas? Is Twitter an appropriate medium for doing so? The problem is likely to be how to get to the heart of an issue or event without losing a sense of its total importance. This activity should remind a technology-minded generation that there are limitations to today's communication methods. Could you really tweet the entire message of the Bible, for example? Here's my try:

God loved. God judged. God sent his Son. God forgave.

Badge making

Badges are important to young people, so it could be good to challenge pupils to make a badge that fits a theme. A successful badge will use a slogan and an image to explain or grab attention for an important statement of faith.

Use the white card badges that can be bought from good stationers; alternatively, provide larger sheets of card, which pupils can cut to the size and shape that best suits their designs. The best badges could be laminated and used in subsequent lessons as examples.

Acrostics

Acrostics can be a useful way to help pupils remember things. An acrostic works by linking the letters of a word in a way that reflects a pattern. For example, some of the Psalms have each verse starting with consecutive letters of the Hebrew alphabet.

This acrostic explains the idea of grace in Christianity:

- **G**od's
- **R**eal
- **A**ctive love at
- **C**hrist's
- **E**xpense

Alphabets

Young children are often given a book containing 26 illustrations that are intended to help them learn the alphabet (for example, starting, 'A is for apple...') One comedian remarked that he was surprised to find that 'xylophone' was one of the most important words in the world, as we have to try to learn it so early!

You could use the alphabet to list key facts about Christianity, starting with the following:

- **A** is for Alpha, the beginning that God is.
- **B** is for Bethlehem, where Jesus was born.
- **C** is for church, where Christians meet together to pray and worship God.
- **D** is for disciple, a follower of Jesus.

Jesus mind map

Ask pupils to design a mind map about the life of Jesus, using a double page in their exercise book. The diagrams should include both notes and labelled drawings to explain major points, and should include the following:

- Where Jesus was born/his early life
- Miracles
- The importance of parables
- Teaching
- Disciples
- Being baptised by John the Baptist
- Palm Sunday—entering the city of Jerusalem on a donkey
- The last supper—giving bread and wine as symbols of his body and blood
- His trial
- The cross
- The resurrection

✛

Glossary of keywords

Adoration   Prayers based on how much people love God.

Baptism   The ritual washing away of sins in Christianity.

Bible   The holy book of Christianity, consisting of two parts: an Old and a New Testament.

Christening   Part of an infant baptism service where the sign of the cross is made on the forehead of a child in order to protect the child from evil.

Christianity   The faith based on the teachings of Jesus Christ.

Church   The community of believing Christians. Can refer to a building where believers meet.

Confession   A type of prayer in which a person says 'sorry' to God for wrong things they have done. Some Christians might confess to a priest to help them receive God's forgiveness.

Confirmation   A service in some Christian churches where people who were baptised as infants confirm their own desire to be followers of Christ.

Cross   The symbol of Christianity, adopted because Jesus was executed on a cross.

God the Father   The first person of the Trinity, seen as being active in creation and as sending the Son and the Holy Spirit to be with people.

Holy Spirit   The third person of the Trinity, who can live in the life of a believer.

Intercession   Prayer asking God to help change situations or people.

Jesus   The founder of Christianity. His name means 'Saviour'.

Marriage   Ceremony designed to bring a husband and wife together according to Christian teaching.

Miracle	A supernatural act; an act of God to change a reality.
Parable	A story with a moral, often used by Jesus in his teaching.
Passover	The Jewish festival that remembers the Jewish escape from slavery in Egypt at the time of Moses.
Pentecost	The Jewish festival that remembers the giving of the law to Moses. In Christianity, it is linked with the giving of the Holy Spirit to believers.
Prayer	Talking and listening to God.
Sin	An act of disobedience to God, which is evil and often hurts others.
Son of God	The title often given to Jesus by Christians to explain that he was from God the Father and the Holy Spirit, as well as a human being. The second person of the Trinity.
Testament	A legal term meaning 'agreement'. The Bible is divided into two Testaments or parts, each of which tells of God's acts in history.
Thanksgiving	Saying thanks to God for his blessings.
Trinity	The idea that God is three persons in one.
Worship	Praising God for who he is and what he has done, in song, prayer or any other way.

✝

Suggested resources

A well-run RE department should develop a collection of helpful artefacts. The impression given by the use of the right artefact can be profound, but so can the use of a less appropriate one. The following is a list of artefacts related to Christianity that would be very useful to have, in order to help pupils to understand the religion. They can be obtained by visiting churches or contacting a retailer such as Articles of Faith (www.articlesoffaith.co.uk), which has produced an extensive catalogue. Local churches might be willing to supply some items or loan them to you while you are studying Christianity.

It is good to provide objects that pupils can touch or focus attention on when undertaking a longer study. Above all, try to select items that show a diversity of Christian beliefs and practices. Let your pupils know that they are living in a world where there are a number of different styles of worship. Make sure they understand that 'Christian' is an umbrella term, covering a good many different ideas.

- Icons
- Crucifixes: obtain a selection, to stimulate pupil reflection on the different messages they send about the cross and Christian belief
- Palm cross
- Bible
- Bible reading notes (to show how Christians try to apply their understanding of the Bible to their daily lives)
- Prayer books: collect a good range, including Church of England, Roman Catholic and Methodist books
- Rosary: the cross and the beads will show pupils how prayer can be a physical activity as well as a spiritual one

- Fish badge (a symbol of the Christian faith)
- Advent calendar: make sure that it is overtly Christian, as many pupils might link Advent calendars simply with chocolate
- Dove symbol (the image of the Holy Spirit)
- Baptismal shell
- Crib with figures
- Chalice: provide photographs of a variety of types
- Statue of the Virgin Mary
- Festal candles (for Christmas, Easter and Pentecost)
- Selection of Christmas cards (religious and non-religious)
- Salvation Army flag
- Postcards of the Holy Land (to give pupils a visual understanding of the places linked with Jesus)
- Postcards of the Vatican
- Images of the Turin Shroud
- CD of traditional and contemporary worship music: music is an important way both to evoke emotion and to illustrate the power of worship
- Hymn books

Enjoyed

this book?

Write a review–we'd love to hear what you think.
Email: reviews@brf.org.uk

Keep up to date–receive details of our new books as they happen.
Sign up for email news and select your interest groups at:
www.brfonline.org.uk/findoutmore/

Follow us on Twitter @brfonline

By post–to receive new title information by post (UK only), complete the form below and post to: BRF Mailing Lists, 15 The Chambers, Vineyard, Abingdon, Oxfordshire, OX14 3FE

Your Details
Name _____
Address_____
_____
Town/City _____ Post Code _____
Email_____

Your Interest Groups (*Please tick as appropriate)	
❏ Advent/Lent	❏ Messy Church
❏ Bible Reading & Study	❏ Pastoral
❏ Children's Books	❏ Prayer & Spirituality
❏ Discipleship	❏ Resources for Children's Church
❏ Leadership	❏ Resources for Schools

Support your local bookshop
Ask about their new title information schemes.